ANNE WILLAN'S
LOOK&COOK
Asian Cooking

ANNE WILLAN'S
LOOK&COOK

Asian Cooking

Recipe Consultant: Lucy Wing

DORLING KINDERSLEY
LONDON • NEW YORK • STUTTGART

DK

A DORLING KINDERSLEY BOOK

Created and Produced by
CARROLL & BROWN LIMITED
5 Lonsdale Road
London NW6 6RA

Editorial Director Jeni Wright
Editors Martha Holmberg
Anna Brandenburger

Art Editor Vicky Zentner
Designer Lucy De Rosa
Production Editor Wendy Rogers

First American Edition, 1994
10 9 8 7 6 5 4 3 2 1

Published in the United States by
Dorling Kindersley, Inc., 232 Madison Avenue
New York, New York 10016

Willan, Anne.
    Asian cooking / by Anne Willan. – 1st American ed.
      p.   cm. – (Anne Willan's Look and cook)
    Includes index.
    ISBN 1-56458-593-X
    1. Cookery (Oriental)   I. Title.   II. Series: Willan, Anne.
Look & cook.
TX724.5.A1W46   1994
641.5951 – dc20   93-37150
                                                                      CIP

Reproduced by Colourscan, Singapore
Printed and bound in Italy by A. Mondadori, Verona

CONTENTS

ASIAN COOKING
THE LOOK & COOK APPROACH

Welcome to **Asian Cooking** and the *Look & Cook* series. These volumes are designed to be the simplest, most informative cookbooks you'll ever own. They are the closest I can come to sharing my personal techniques for cooking my own favorite recipes without actually being with you in the kitchen looking over your shoulder.

Equipment and ingredients often determine whether or not you can cook a particular dish, so *Look & Cook* illustrates everything you need at the beginning of each recipe. You'll see at a glance how long a recipe takes to cook, how many servings it makes, what the finished dish looks like, and how much preparation can be done ahead. When you start to cook, you'll find the preparation and cooking are organized into steps that are easy to follow. Each stage has its own color coding and everything is shown in photographs with brief text to go with each step. You will never be in doubt as to what it is you are doing, why you are doing it, and how it should look.

EQUIPMENT

INGREDIENTS

🍽 SERVES 4-6   🥢 WORK TIME 25-35 MINUTES   ☕ COOKING TIME 20-30 MINUTES

I've also included helpful hints and ideas under "Anne Says." These may list an alternative ingredient or piece of equipment, or explain a certain method, or add some advice on mastering a particular technique. Similarly, if there is a crucial stage in a recipe when things can go astray, I've included some warnings called "Take Care."

Many of the photographs are annotated to pinpoint why certain pieces of equipment work best, and how food should look at the various stages of cooking. Because presentation is so important, a picture of the finished dish with serving suggestions is at the end of each recipe.

Thanks to all this information you can't go wrong. I'll be with you every step of the way. So please come with me into the kitchen to look, cook, and enjoy some **Asian Cooking**.

WHY ASIAN COOKING?

The area loosely termed "Asia" covers a vast part of the globe, and the countries encompassed are equally varied in geography, language, and culture. There is, however, a thread of similarity running through the cuisines of these countries. Population movements within Asia have carried culinary preferences and customs from region to region. Climates are generally hot and tropical so countries share similar indigenous fruits, vegetables, and herbs.

Throughout Asia there is respect for ingredients. An Asian cook selects only the freshest items, then takes care to preserve and highlight their essential nature when cooking with them. Careful food preparation and service is also of great importance in Asian cultures, and is seen as a worthwhile use of time. Great attention is paid to presentation, and the meal is an opportunity for family and friends to gather and socialize.

China is the largest of all Asian countries, and the most diverse in terms of geography and culture. In the cold northern climate, wheat is a staple, leading to robust simple dishes, such as dumplings, noodles, and pancakes. Further east around Shanghai, the climate is mild and the land fertile. Dishes are delicate and often slightly sweet, with fish and shellfish from the Yangtze River and the East China Sea featuring prominently. The cuisine of Western Szechwan is typified by hot chili peppers and sour, sweet, and salty combinations, while food from the semi-tropical area near Guangdong is milder, sensuous, and savory, with the many dim sum delicacies as a prime example. Historically, Japan has been isolated from the influences of other countries, so its cuisine stands apart. Deceptively simple, the elements of a Japanese meal are subtle, with ingredients such as seafood, sea vegetables, tofu, and soy sauce blending together in delicious sophistication.

In contrast, the flavors of Korea are more pungent, with garlic, ginger, pepper, scallions, sesame, and soy sauce used in generous quantities. Pickled vegetables are indispensable to a Korean meal, with pickled cabbage (kimchee) being the most popular accompaniment.

The Southeast Asian countries of Thailand, Indonesia, and Malaysia each have their own cuisine, but certain elements are common to all. Vibrant, colorful presentations are the norm. Assertive, complex flavors are created by blending ingredients into spice pastes. Common ingredients include chili peppers, lemon grass, coconut milk, tamarind, shrimp paste, and galangal.

The cuisine of Vietnam, also in Southeast Asia, stands somewhat apart from its neighbors, with less emphasis on heat and more on the subtle blending of herbs and spices, with an occasional hint of its French colonial past. Salty fish sauce is used in almost every dish, while fresh coriander and mint, lemon grass, star anise, and cinnamon appear frequently in Vietnamese recipes.

The sections on Equipment, Techniques, and Ingredients, in this volume give you the practical know-how you'll need to create the flavors of these Asian cuisines, and the Glossary gives you back-up information. From cleavers to woks, and bamboo shoots to wasabi, we'll show you the way.

RECIPE CHOICE

No wonder we're fascinated by Asian cooking. Its ancient history and vitality today make it one of the most dynamic influences on dining tables set around the world. The recipes included in this volume are traditional offerings, some with contemporary twists.

SOUPS AND SMALL DISHES

Clear Soup with Shrimp and Spinach (Ebi no Suimono): colorful ingredients are artistically prepared and arranged in a subtle Japanese soup stock. *Clear Soup with Sea Bass (Suzuki no Suimono):* this delicate soup featuring chunks of fresh sea bass, wedges of crisp, spicy daikon, and watercress is served in winter in Japan. *Beef Noodle Soup (Pho Bac):* a hearty soup boasting oxtail meat, slices of raw beef, rice noodles, and bean sprouts, in a rich beef broth perfumed with star anise and cinnamon. *Beef and Rice Soup (Chao Thit Bo):* chopped beef and rice fortify the broth in this Vietnamese meal-in-a-bowl. *Fried Potstickers (Jaozi):* a favorite *dim sum* dish, these little dumplings are stuffed with a gingery pork and cabbage filling, shallow-fried for a crispy bottom, then steamed until tender. *Steamed Open-Faced Dumplings (Shao Mai):* a savory pork and cabbage mixture fills little pouch-like Cantonese dumplings that are steamed to perfection in a bamboo steamer. *Thai Skewered Chicken (Gai Satay):* nuggets of chicken are soaked in a coconut milk marinade, golden with turmeric, then skewered and broiled to serve with a sweet-spicy sauce and chili-cucumber salad. *Japanese Chicken Kebabs (Yakitori):* skewers of scallions and chicken are brushed with a sweet soy sauce glaze during broiling. *Vietnamese Spring Rolls (Gio Cuon):* little bundles of shrimp and pork salad, wrapped up in sheets of chewy rice paper, to dunk in a sauce brimming with hot, sweet, and sour flavors. *Vegetarian Spring Rolls (Gio Chey):* an earthy-flavored snack, these rolls are filled with dried mushrooms, accompanied by a rich version of hoisin sauce. *Vinegared Rice Rolled in Seaweed (Nori-Maki):* tender rice encases strips of sweet raw tuna and crisp cucumber, spiked with a dash of green horseradish, then rolled in a thin sheet of roasted seaweed. *Rice Mounds Topped with Shrimp (Nigiri-Sushi):* cooked jumbo shrimp are butterflied and top bite-sized ovals of rice – truly elegant finger-food!

LARGE DISHES

Steamed Fish in Black Bean Sauce (Zang Yu Dau Shi): whole red snapper is steamed with fermented black beans, garlic, ginger root, and soy sauce and decorated with scallion brushes. *Lemon Grass and Basil Scented Steamed Fish (Ooh Pla):* fresh Thai flavors permeate this quick and easy dish of steamed snapper. *Spiced Seafood Salad (Yum Pla Talay):* white fish, squid, shrimp, and scallops are poached and tossed in a lime juice, garlic, and kaffir lime leaf dressing. *Spiced Seafood and Chilled Noodle Salad:* cellophane noodles dressed with sesame oil and lime form a nest for marinated seafood. *Japanese One-Pot Meal (Yosenabe):* a pot full of simmering *dashi* stock, chock-full of good things – oysters, clams, chicken, noodles, and vegetables. *Braised Beef and Vegetables (Sukiyaki):* lean beef is seared then braised with tofu, shiitake mushrooms, noodles, and vegetables in a cast-iron *sukiyaki* pan. *Lemon Grass Chicken (Ga Xao Xa Ot):* balmy lemon grass and mild chili peppers team up to flavor this quick stir-fry, served on a fresh green salad. *Lemon Grass Pork (Moo Paht Tak Rai):* strips of tender pork loin are stir-fried with lemon grass, garlic, and chili peppers, then served on a bed of rice. *Chinese Roast Duck (Shao Ya):* a special drying technique produces crispy skin and juicy meat, strikingly presented in this Chinese masterpiece. *Cantonese Roast Chicken (Shao Ji):* a whole plump chicken is roasted in a sweet and savory glaze. *Yellow Flower Pork (Mu Shu Rou):* delicate strips of omelet are stir-fried with pork, dried Chinese mushrooms, tree ears, and tiger lily buds, then wrapped at the table in thin pancakes flavored with a hint of sesame oil. *Yellow Flower Vegetables (Mu Shu Th'ai):* crispy fried strips of tofu replace the pork in this vegetarian stir-fried favorite. *Indonesian Curried Beef (Rendang Daging):* chunks of beef are simmered until meltingly tender in a coconut and spice sauce, to create a typical Indonesian dry curry. *Vietnamese Stewed Beef (Thit Bo Kno):* beef chunks are marinated in ginger root, lemon grass, and chili peppers, browned, then simmered in a broth fragrant with star anise. *Korean Grilled Beef (Bulgogi):* hot and sour pickled vegetables accompany marinated strips of beef tenderloin, grilled on a table-top burner.

RICE, NOODLE, AND VEGETABLE DISHES

Malaysian Fried Rice Noodles (Char Kway Teow): a hearty main course stir-fry of rice noodles, sausage, shrimp, and eggs. *Thai Fried Noodles (Pad Thai):* pungent tamarind and intensely salty dried shrimp give a truly authentic flavor to this Thai favorite. *Indonesian Fried Rice (Nasi Goreng):* chicken and shrimp star in this stir-fried rice dish, heady with shrimp paste, hot pepper flakes, and sweet soy sauce. *Thai Curry Fried Rice (Kao Pad):* curry powder, cumin, and coriander add spice to this stir-fried chicken and rice dish. *Buddha's Delight (Lo Han Chai):* vegetarian or not, you'll delight at this meatless dish of crunchy exotic vegetables, noodles, and tofu. *Vietnamese Vegetarian Stir-Fry (La Han Chay):* green beans, cauliflower, and carrots are tossed with noodles and strips of fried tofu with a deep, woody touch from dried Chinese black mushrooms and tree ears. *Mixed Pickled Vegetables (Acar):* vibrant with color and flavor, this dish features assorted vegetables blanched and tossed in a pickling sauce with macadamia nuts. *Vegetable and Tofu Salad in Peanut Sauce:* tangy peanut sauce coats vegetables and tofu in this main-dish salad.

SWEET DISHES

Almond Milk Curd with Fresh Fruit (Xian Guo Xan Ren Dou Fu): almond-infused sweetened milk is set with unflavored gelatin and cut into attractive diamond shapes to serve with exotic lychees and juicy tangerine sections in syrup as a perfect light dessert. *Almond Milk Curd with Plums and Almonds (Xan Ren Dou Fu Lizi Xan Ren):* tiny cubes of almond milk curd are served with juicy plums and crunchy toasted almonds. *Banana Fritters with Lime and Caramel Syrup (Kluay Tord):* deep-fried until golden brown, coconut-coated bananas are served with a tangy lime-caramel syrup. *Apple Fritters with Caramel Syrup and Sesame:* crisp wedges of apple are dipped in batter, deep-fried, and sprinkled with crunchy sesame seeds. *Sticky Rice with Mangoes (Khao Niew Mamuang):* coconut-rich rice pudding is accented by the bright tropical taste of juicy mango slices. *Sticky Rice with Fresh Pineapple and Coconut:* fresh pineapple slices and toasted shredded coconut complement this sticky rice dessert made with creamy coconut.

PRESENTING AN ASIAN MEAL

A typical Asian meal does not feature one main dish supported by appetizers and side dishes, but rather it is composed of an array of dishes all presented at the same time to create a welcoming feeling of abundance – a multi-course meal. Only in Japan is the pace of the meal closer to the Western style, one course at a time, served in individual rather than communal portions. Noodles or rice are the principle element on every Asian table, served as a bland but nourishing backdrop for the other more lively dishes. Start by spooning some rice onto a plate, then add small portions from the meat, fish, poultry, or vegetable dishes, and top with condiments, such as soy sauce, fish sauce, or pickled vegetables. In Japan, rice forms a less integral part of the meal, usually served toward the end, and not always mixed with the other dishes.

A soup may be included, as an opener in Japanese style, or possibly sipped throughout the meal, or used to moisten the rice. Asian meals rarely end with a dessert, although they are popular in Malaysia. Fresh fruit may be offered as a refreshing finale, but usually sweet dishes are eaten as snacks during the day.

Although chopsticks are the primary implement in China, Japan, Vietnam, and Korea, in Malaysia, Indonesia, and Thailand, fingers are the traditional – and polite – means of conveying food from the plate to your mouth. You'll find that Western-style spoons and forks are routinely laid on dining tables in these countries. The goal in constructing any Asian meal, whether a full-scale banquet or a simple supper around the family table, is to create a harmonious mix of flavors and textures. Choose a good balance of meat, fish, or poultry, according to your taste, and always have plenty of vegetables. Consider the contrast of textures, which are far more varied than in Western cooking. Avoid, for instance, too many fried dishes. And always include plenty of noodles or rice, whether fluffy as served in Indonesia, Malaysia, Thailand, and Vietnam, or slightly sticky as preferred in China, Korea, and Japan. Rice should always be perfectly cooked, and piping hot.

CLEAR SOUP WITH SHRIMP AND SPINACH

Ebi no Suimono

🍽 SERVES 4 🥣 WORK TIME 40–50 MINUTES

EQUIPMENT

saucepans

colander

bamboo rolling mat†

paper towels

bowls

chopsticks

chef's knife

cheesecloth

small knife

vegetable peeler

slotted spoon

strainer

ladle

chopping board

INGREDIENTS

Asian spinach†

carrot

dried bonito flakes

dried kelp

raw shrimp

cornstarch

Japanese rice wine ‡

Japanese soy sauce

†regular spinach can also be used

‡dry sherry can also be used

Almost every Japanese meal includes a soup, ranging from a classic miso (fermented bean paste) soup to a thick broth that is a meal in itself. This simple clear soup, based on the fish- and seaweed-flavored stock, dashi, *exemplifies the effective presentation so characteristic of Japanese cooking. Serve it piping hot in covered Japanese bowls.*

GETTING AHEAD

The soup stock can be made up to 2 days ahead and kept, covered, in the refrigerator. Its delicate flavor does not hold up to freezing.

SHOPPING LIST

¹/₂	small carrot
4 oz	Asian spinach
	salt
8	raw, unpeeled large shrimp, total weight about ¹/₂ lb
2 tbsp	Japanese rice wine
1 tbsp	cornstarch
1 tsp	Japanese soy sauce
	For the soup stock
1 quart	cold water
4-inch	piece of dried kelp
¹/₃ cup	loosely packed dried bonito flakes

ORDER OF WORK

1 PREPARE THE SOUP STOCK

2 PREPARE THE VEGETABLES

3 MAKE THE SHRIMP FLOWERS

4 FINISH THE SOUP

† aluminum foil can also be used

1 PREPARE THE SOUP STOCK

1 Put the cold water in a large saucepan and add the dried kelp.

2 Bring the water to a boil over high heat, then immediately remove the kelp with the chopsticks or slotted spoon and discard it. Remove the pan from the heat.

! TAKE CARE !
Remove the kelp as soon as the water comes to a boil; if it is allowed to boil, the stock will be bitter and cloudy.

Dried kelp flavors water quickly

3 Sprinkle the dried bonito flakes evenly over the surface of the kelp-infused water.

Straining through cheesecloth helps produce clear stock

Discard bonito flakes after straining

4 Let the stock stand until the flakes settle to the bottom, 3–5 minutes, depending on how thick and dry the flakes are.

ANNE SAYS
"Unlike other soup stocks that need long simmering, Japanese stock is quickly made, producing a clear, subtly flavored liquid with a hint of the sea."

5 Line the strainer with damp cheesecloth. Strain the stock through the cheesecloth.

ANNE SAYS
"Damp cheesecloth will not shed lint or fibers during straining, and will produce a clear, pure stock."

2 PREPARE THE VEGETABLES

Young tender spinach leaves are used for soup

1 Discard the tough stems and ribs from the spinach leaves and wash them thoroughly.

2 Trim the carrot and peel it with the vegetable peeler. Cut the carrot crosswise into 8 slices.

Spinach will cook very quickly in boiling water

3 Half-fill a medium saucepan with water, add a pinch of salt, and bring to a boil. Add the carrot slices and simmer until tender, 3–5 minutes. Lift them out of the water, using the slotted spoon, and set aside.

4 Return the water to a boil and add the spinach. Simmer until tender, 2–3 minutes.

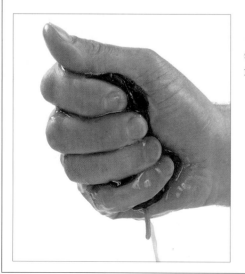

5 Drain the spinach in the colander and rinse with cold water. Gently squeeze the spinach in your fist to remove excess water.

6 Unfold the tangled spinach leaves and open them so they are as flat as possible.

ANNE SAYS
"Work carefully to avoid tearing the spinach leaves. If tears do occur, just piece the leaves together when stacking them on the mat."

7 Carefully stack the spinach leaves on the bamboo rolling mat to form a 4-inch square.

8 Lift the end of the mat and roll up the spinach square firmly to a 1-inch cylinder, squeezing out any more water.

Bamboo mat is handy for rolling up spinach leaves

9 Transfer the spinach roll to the cutting board. With the chef's knife, cut the roll across into 4 equal pieces and set them aside until ready to finish the soup.

3 MAKE THE SHRIMP FLOWERS

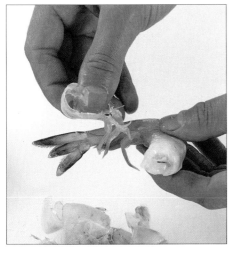

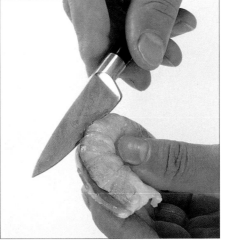

1 With your fingers, peel off the shells from the shrimp.

2 Using the small knife, make a shallow cut along the back of each peeled shrimp.

3 Discard the dark intestinal vein from the shrimp. Rinse the shrimp under cold running water, and pat dry with paper towels.

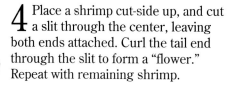

Curl tail through center slit

4 Place a shrimp cut-side up, and cut a slit through the center, leaving both ends attached. Curl the tail end through the slit to form a "flower." Repeat with remaining shrimp.

5 Put the prepared shrimp in a small bowl, add the rice wine, and lightly toss together with your fingers so the shrimp are all moistened.

6 Bring a medium saucepan of water to a boil. Put the cornstarch on a small plate. Holding each shrimp by the tail, dredge all sides in the cornstarch.

7 Drop the shrimp into the pan of boiling water and cook until they just turn pink, 1–2 minutes. Transfer the shrimp with the chopsticks or slotted spoon to a plate and set aside.

4 **FINISH THE SOUP**

1 Bring the soup stock to a boil with the soy sauce, adding more to taste. Arrange 2 shrimp flowers and 1 piece of spinach roll, cut-side up, in 4 warmed soup bowls.

Hot soup is carefully ladled into bowls over garnish ingredients

2 Carefully ladle in the boiling soup, taking care not to disturb the shrimp and spinach arrangement.

3 Gently drop 2 of the prepared carrot slices into the center of each soup bowl. Place bowls on bamboo trays or plates for easy serving.

🍴 TO SERVE
The Japanese hold the soup bowl in one hand and use the chopsticks for picking up the solid ingredients. No soup spoon is used with clear soups – the soup stock is sipped directly from the bowl.

Japanese suimono is delicately flavored and beautifully presented

Carrot rounds highlight pink of shrimp

VARIATION
CLEAR SOUP WITH SEA BASS
SUZUKI NO SUIMONO

In this soup, white radish – daikon – is cut and cooked in place of spinach, while fish chunks replace the shrimp. In Japan, this hearty soup is served in the winter.

1 Omit the large shrimp and Asian spinach.
2 Make the soup stock and cook the carrot slices as directed.

3 Cut a cleaned sea bass (about ³/₄ lb) across into 4 steaks, discarding the head and tail. Toss the fish with 1 tbsp Japanese rice wine, then simmer in boiling water just until firm, 2–3 minutes. Drain, and reserve.

4 With a vegetable peeler, peel a 1-inch piece of daikon; cut it into 8 wedges. Half-fill a small saucepan with water, add a pinch of salt and the daikon, and bring to a boil. Simmer the daikon just until tender, 8–10 minutes. Drain and set it aside.
5 Using the vegetable peeler, pare 2–3 strips of zest from 1 lemon; cut the zest into 12 strips.
6 Heat the soup stock and add the soy sauce as directed. Arrange the fish and vegetables in 4 warmed soup bowls. Ladle the stock over the ingredients as directed. Sprinkle each soup bowl with 3 strips of lemon zest and decorate with a sprig of fresh watercress.

BEEF NOODLE SOUP

Pho Bac

🍽️ SERVES 4   🥣 WORK TIME 1½ HOURS*   ♨️ COOKING TIME 4–5 HOURS

EQUIPMENT

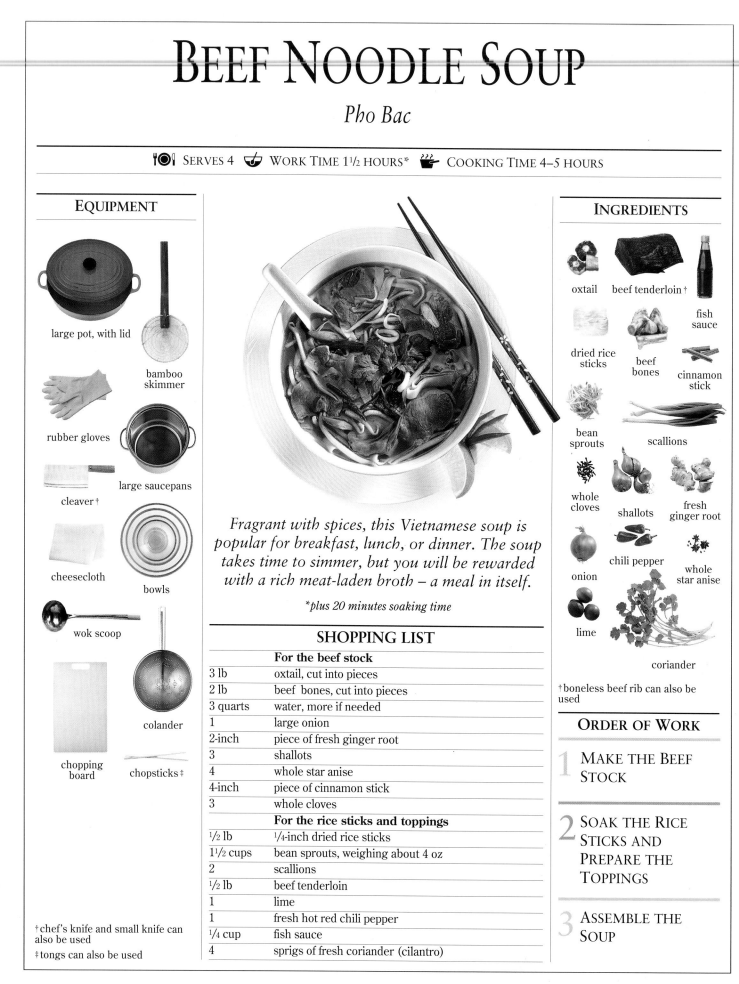

large pot, with lid

bamboo skimmer

rubber gloves

cleaver †

large saucepans

cheesecloth

bowls

wok scoop

chopping board

chopsticks ‡

colander

† chef's knife and small knife can also be used

‡ tongs can also be used

Fragrant with spices, this Vietnamese soup is popular for breakfast, lunch, or dinner. The soup takes time to simmer, but you will be rewarded with a rich meat-laden broth – a meal in itself.

*plus 20 minutes soaking time

INGREDIENTS

oxtail   beef tenderloin †

fish sauce

dried rice sticks   beef bones   cinnamon stick

bean sprouts   scallions

whole cloves   shallots   fresh ginger root

onion   chili pepper   whole star anise

lime   coriander

† boneless beef rib can also be used

ORDER OF WORK

1 MAKE THE BEEF STOCK

2 SOAK THE RICE STICKS AND PREPARE THE TOPPINGS

3 ASSEMBLE THE SOUP

SHOPPING LIST

	For the beef stock	
3 lb	oxtail, cut into pieces	
2 lb	beef bones, cut into pieces	
3 quarts	water, more if needed	
1	large onion	
2-inch	piece of fresh ginger root	
3	shallots	
4	whole star anise	
4-inch	piece of cinnamon stick	
3	whole cloves	
	For the rice sticks and toppings	
½ lb	¼-inch dried rice sticks	
1½ cups	bean sprouts, weighing about 4 oz	
2	scallions	
½ lb	beef tenderloin	
1	lime	
1	fresh hot red chili pepper	
¼ cup	fish sauce	
4	sprigs of fresh coriander (cilantro)	

1 MAKE THE BEEF STOCK

Gelatin in oxtail and beef bones is essential for good stock

1 Put the oxtail and beef bones in the large pot. Add water to cover; bring to a boil. Simmer, 10 minutes.

2 Drain the oxtail and bones in the colander and rinse with cold water.

ANNE SAYS
"Blanching and rinsing cleans the bones so they will produce less scum while simmering."

3 Rinse the pot and return the oxtail and bones to it. Add the 3 quarts water, cover, and bring slowly to a boil.

4 Meanwhile, heat the broiler. With the cleaver, cut the unpeeled onion lengthwise in half, then cut the unpeeled piece of ginger root crosswise into pieces.

Broiling vegetables mellows their flavor

Vegetables are browned in their skins to add more flavor

5 Arrange the onion halves and ginger pieces on the broiler rack. Add the unpeeled shallots. Broil 3–4 inches from the heat until well browned, 3–5 minutes.

6 Turn the vegetables and brown the other sides, 3–5 minutes.

ANNE SAYS
"You can also use a cast-iron skillet for browning."

7 Add the browned vegetables to the pot with the star anise, cinnamon stick, and cloves.

8 Cover, and simmer over low heat until the oxtail pieces are tender, 3–4 hours. Add more water if needed, to keep the bones covered. Occasionally skim the fat from the surface with the wok scoop.

Lift oxtail pieces from stock so meat can be removed

9 Using the bamboo skimmer, remove the oxtail pieces from the stock. Set them aside.

10 When cool enough to handle, remove the meat from the oxtail bones with your fingers and reserve.

11 Return the oxtail bones to the stock, and continue simmering the stock, 1 hour longer.

Dampened cheesecloth absorbs less stock

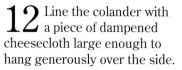

12 Line the colander with a piece of dampened cheesecloth large enough to hang generously over the side.

13 Strain the stock into a large saucepan. Discard the bones and vegetables.

Fat in bowl should be discarded

14 Skim off all the fat, taste the stock for seasoning, and set it aside. You should have about 2 quarts.

2 SOAK THE RICE STICKS AND PREPARE THE TOPPINGS

1 Put the rice sticks in a bowl, and cover with warm water. Let soak until soft, about 20 minutes.

2 Pick over the bean sprouts, and discard any that are brown or wilted.

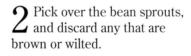

Arrange beef slices in single layer so they do not stick together

3 Trim the scallions, leaving some of the green tops, and cut them into diagonal slices.

4 With the cleaver, cut the beef across the grain into very thin slices. Arrange the slices of beef on a tray, cover tightly, and refrigerate until finishing the soup.

Slice with stroking motion for thinnest possible slices

ANNE SAYS
"You can freeze the meat for easier slicing, 30 minutes."

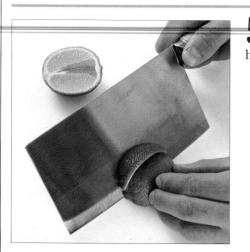

5 With the cleaver, cut the lime lengthwise in half, then cut each half into 4 wedges.

6 Wearing rubber gloves, cut the chili pepper lengthwise in half, discarding the core. Scrape out the seeds and cut away the fleshy white ribs from each half. Cut each half into very thin strips.

3 ASSEMBLE THE SOUP

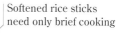

Softened rice sticks need only brief cooking

1 Add the oxtail meat and fish sauce to the stock, and bring to a boil. Remove the beef from the refrigerator.

2 Half-fill a large pan with water and bring to a boil. Drain the rice sticks, add to the boiling water, and stir. Return the water to a boil; drain again.

Soaked rice sticks will cook very quickly in boiling water

3 Using the chopsticks or slotted spoon, divide the rice sticks equally among 4 large soup bowls.

4 Top the rice sticks with the bean sprouts, raw beef slices, and scallions.

5 Carefully ladle some of the boiling beef stock with some of the oxtail meat into each bowl.

ANNE SAYS
"The boiling beef stock will cook the raw beef slices."

🍽 TO SERVE
Serve the soup at once, while it is very hot, decorated with coriander sprigs. Allow each diner to add chili pepper strips and lime, to taste.

Bean sprouts and scallions add crunchy texture

VARIATION

BEEF AND RICE SOUP
CHAO THIT BO
This basic soup is popular all over Vietnam. Sometimes the meat is shaped into balls.

1 Omit rice sticks, bean sprouts, lime, and chili pepper. Prepare the stock as directed, omitting the star anise, cinnamon, and cloves.
2 Soak 1 oz cellophane noodles in warm water, 20 minutes. Drain, and cut into 2-inch lengths.
3 Meanwhile, peel 1 small onion and cut it lengthwise in half. Set each half cut-side down; slice horizontally, then vertically, toward the root, leaving the slices attached. Cut across into dice. Continue chopping until very fine.

Thinly sliced beef and rich stock are the basis of a hearty soup

4 Cut the beef into $1/2$-inch slices. Cut the slices lengthwise into strips, then across into dice. Continue chopping until very fine. Mix the beef and onion with 1 tbsp fish sauce and $1/4$ tsp ground black pepper, cover, and refrigerate.
5 In a large saucepan, heat 1 tbsp vegetable oil over medium heat. Add $2/3$ cup long-grain rice and cook, stirring, about 1 minute.
6 Add the strained beef stock and oxtail meat, and bring to a boil over high heat. Cover, and simmer over low heat just until tender, about 20 minutes.
7 Slice the scallions as directed. Chop 2 tbsp unsalted roasted peanuts.
8 Stir the soaked noodles into the soup, with 3 tbsp fish sauce and 2 tsp sugar, and bring back to a boil. Taste for seasoning, adding more fish sauce or pepper if necessary.
9 Put the chopped beef mixture in warmed soup bowls and ladle in the soup. Use chopsticks to stir the soup. Sprinkle with scallions and chopped peanuts, and decorate with coriander sprigs.

GETTING AHEAD
The stock can be made ahead and refrigerated up to 3 days, or frozen. The toppings can be prepared up to 4 hours ahead and kept, covered, in the refrigerator. Slice the beef, soak the rice sticks, and reheat the stock just before serving.

FRIED POTSTICKERS

Jaozi

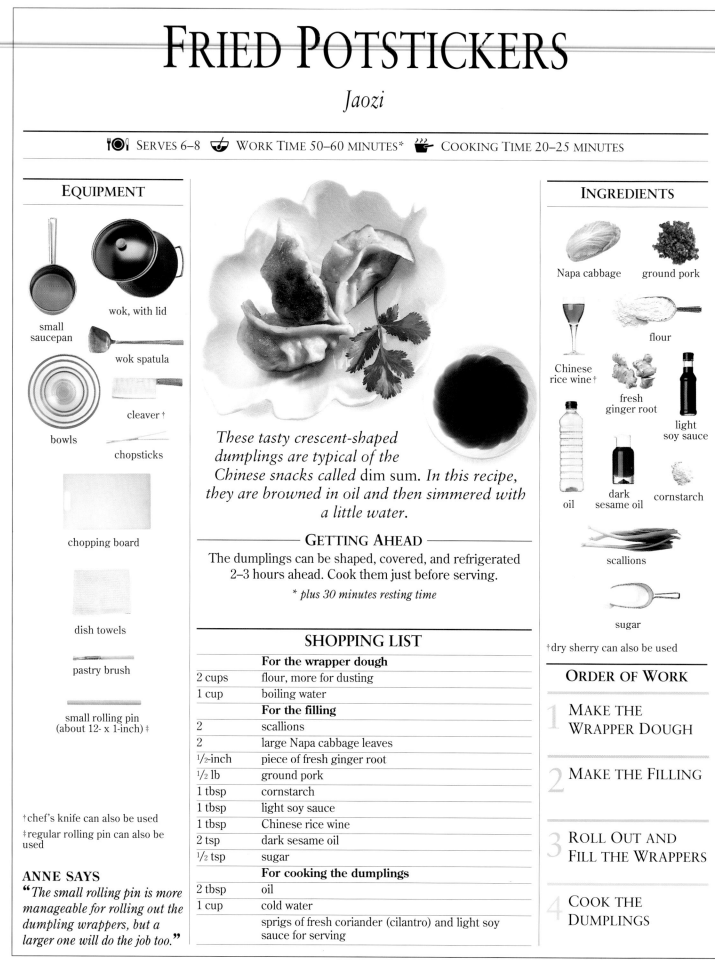

EQUIPMENT

small saucepan

wok, with lid

wok spatula

cleaver †

bowls

chopsticks

chopping board

dish towels

pastry brush

small rolling pin
(about 12- x 1-inch) ‡

†chef's knife can also be used

‡regular rolling pin can also be used

ANNE SAYS

"*The small rolling pin is more manageable for rolling out the dumpling wrappers, but a larger one will do the job too.*"

These tasty crescent-shaped dumplings are typical of the Chinese snacks called dim sum. *In this recipe, they are browned in oil and then simmered with a little water.*

GETTING AHEAD

The dumplings can be shaped, covered, and refrigerated 2–3 hours ahead. Cook them just before serving.

* plus 30 minutes resting time

SHOPPING LIST

	For the wrapper dough
2 cups	flour, more for dusting
1 cup	boiling water
	For the filling
2	scallions
2	large Napa cabbage leaves
1/2-inch	piece of fresh ginger root
1/2 lb	ground pork
1 tbsp	cornstarch
1 tbsp	light soy sauce
1 tbsp	Chinese rice wine
2 tsp	dark sesame oil
1/2 tsp	sugar
	For cooking the dumplings
2 tbsp	oil
1 cup	cold water
	sprigs of fresh coriander (cilantro) and light soy sauce for serving

INGREDIENTS

Napa cabbage

ground pork

flour

Chinese rice wine †

fresh ginger root

light soy sauce

oil

dark sesame oil

cornstarch

scallions

sugar

†dry sherry can also be used

ORDER OF WORK

1 MAKE THE WRAPPER DOUGH

2 MAKE THE FILLING

3 ROLL OUT AND FILL THE WRAPPERS

4 COOK THE DUMPLINGS

1 MAKE THE WRAPPER DOUGH

1 Put the flour in a large bowl and make a well in the center. Slowly pour the boiling water into the well, mixing in the flour with the chopsticks.

2 Continue mixing with the chopsticks until the water is absorbed and the mixture forms a rough mass, adding more flour if necessary. Cover the bowl with a dish towel and let stand until cool enough to handle, about 1 minute.

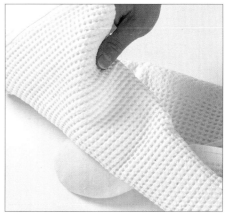

3 When cool, gather up the dough with your hand and press into a loose ball. It should be quite soft.

4 Turn the dough onto a lightly floured surface and knead it, adding more flour if necessary, until it is smooth and elastic, about 5 minutes.

5 Cover with a dish towel, and let it rest, about 30 minutes. Meanwhile, make the filling.

2 MAKE THE FILLING

1 Trim the scallions, leaving some of the green tops. Slice them lengthwise into thin strips.

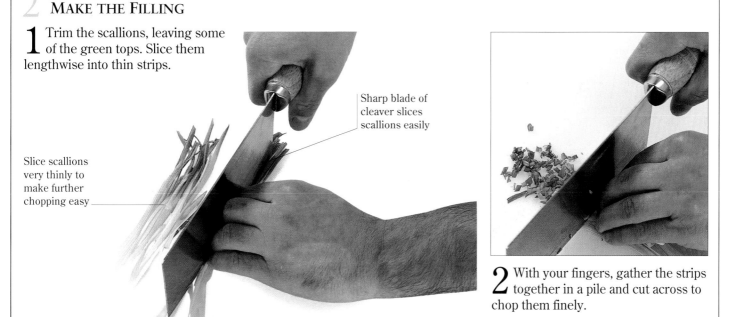

Sharp blade of cleaver slices scallions easily

Slice scallions very thinly to make further chopping easy

2 With your fingers, gather the strips together in a pile and cut across to chop them finely.

Chopsticks are used to blend filling

4 In a large bowl, combine the scallions, cabbage, and ginger with the ground pork, cornstarch, soy sauce, rice wine, sesame oil, and sugar. Mix well, using the chopsticks.

Cabbage and scallions add texture to filling

3 Stack the cabbage leaves. With the cleaver, cut them lengthwise into quarters and then across into 1/8-inch slices. Peel and chop the ginger (see box, below).

HOW TO PEEL, SLICE, AND CHOP FRESH GINGER ROOT

The sharp heavy blade of a cleaver makes quick work of preparing ginger root. A regular chef's knife can also be used, in which case, peel the skin from the ginger root with a vegetable peeler.

Heavy cleaver blade is excellent for scraping off ginger skin

1 With the cleaver, trim off any knobs and scrape the skin from the ginger root.

2 Thinly slice the ginger root, cutting across the fibrous grain.

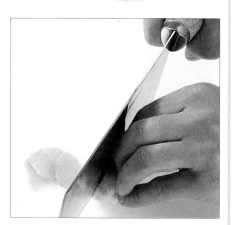

Scraping with cleaver removes minimum of flesh with skin

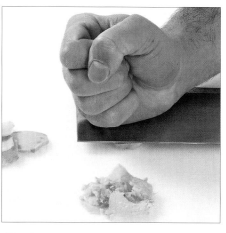

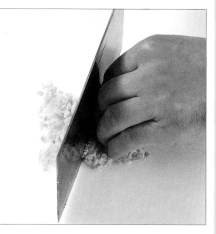

3 Place the cleaver flat on each slice of ginger root, and smash it with your fist to crush the slice.

4 Cut the slices of ginger root into dice, and continue chopping until they become quite fine.

3 ROLL OUT AND FILL THE WRAPPERS

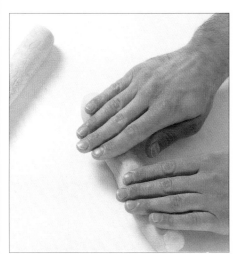

1 Divide the dough in half and, with your fingers, roll each half into a cylinder about 9 inches long.

2 Lightly dust the cleaver with flour, then cut each cylinder across into 12 equal pieces. Cover the pieces with a damp dish towel.

ANNE SAYS
"Keep the pieces of dough and the finished wrappers covered with a damp towel to prevent them from drying out."

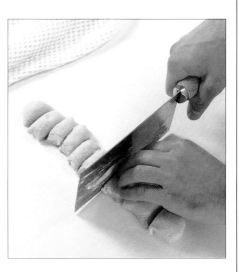

Dough for wrapper is smooth and very pliable

3 Dust your palms with flour, then take one piece of dough and roll it into a ball. Repeat with the remaining dough and cover with the damp dish towel.

Lightly flour your palms so dough does not stick

4 Lightly flour the work surface and rolling pin. Flatten one ball of dough with the palm of your hand, and roll it out to a 4-inch round, making the edges slightly thinner than the center. Cover with a damp dish towel. Repeat with the remaining balls of dough.

5 Set one wrapper on the work surface. Place 1 tablespoon of the filling in the center of the wrapper.

6 Lightly moisten the edge of the wrapper with the pastry brush dipped in water.

! TAKE CARE !
Do not over-moisten the wrapper when brushing with water or the dough will become sticky and difficult to shape.

Light brushing of water helps seal dumpling

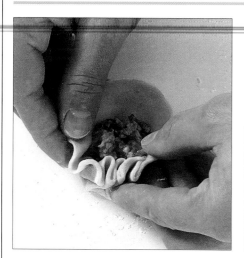
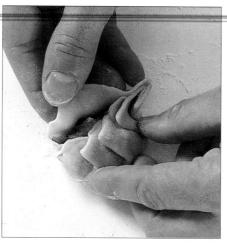

7 Make 5 or 6 pleats along half of the wrapper edge to gather together and enclose the filling mixture.

8 Carefully lift the unpleated edge of the wrapper over the filling to join the pleated edge.

9 Press the edges of the wrapper together with your fingers to seal, bending to curve the seam.

10 Dip the bottom of each dumpling in a little flour and place it on a tray. Cover the tray with a damp dish towel to prevent the dumplings from drying out.

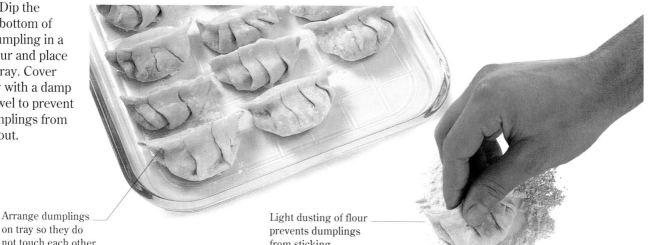

Arrange dumplings on tray so they do not touch each other

Light dusting of flour prevents dumplings from sticking

4 COOK THE DUMPLINGS

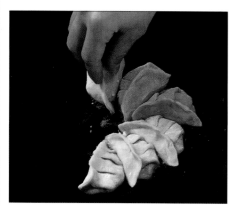

1 Heat the wok over medium heat. Drizzle in half of the oil to coat the bottom and sides of the wok. Continue heating until the oil is very hot. Arrange 12 dumplings flat-side down in the wok in a single layer.

2 Fry the dumplings until they are lightly browned and crisp on the base, 1–2 minutes.

Check underside of dumplings from time to time to ensure they do not scorch

3 Carefully add half of
the cold water and
immediately cover the wok.
Reduce heat to medium-low
and continue to cook until all
the liquid has evaporated and the dumplings are tender but
still chewy, 8–10 minutes. With the wok spatula, transfer the
dumplings to warmed individual plates or a platter and keep
them warm. Repeat to cook the remaining dumplings.

Pour water into
center of wok
so steam will
cook dumplings

🍴 **TO SERVE**
Decorate the dumplings with coriander
sprigs and serve warm, with soy sauce
for dipping.

Potstickers
should be served
hot, brown-side
up if you like

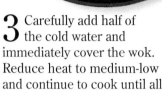

Soy sauce adds a savory
accent to chewy dumplings

V A R I A T I O N
STEAMED OPEN-FACED DUMPLINGS
SHAO MAI

*These Cantonese
dumplings are
a favorite in*
dim sum
teahouses.

1 Make the dough, the filling, and the dumpling wrappers
as directed in the main recipe.
2 Put 1 tablespoon of filling in the center of each wrapper
and brush with water as directed.
3 To shape the dumplings, lift the wrapper up around the
filling, gathering and pinching the wrapper to form a purse.
The top of the filling should be exposed. Squeeze the
wrapper firmly around the middle to secure it.
Put the dumplings on a tray without
dusting with flour, and cover with
a damp towel.
4 Put 2 cups of water in
the wok, cover, and
bring to a boil. Line a
bamboo steamer with
additional Napa
cabbage leaves.
Arrange half of the
dumplings in a single
layer on the cabbage
leaves, cover the steamer
with its lid, and place in
the wok.
5 Steam the dumplings,
until tender but still chewy,
12–15 minutes. Remove
the steamer from the wok and transfer the
dumplings to warmed individual plates and
keep warm. Repeat to steam the remaining
dumplings. Decorate the plates with cabbage
leaves and herbs, if you like. Serve warm,
with soy sauce and hot chili oil for dipping.

VIETNAMESE SPRING ROLLS

Gio Cuon

🍽 SERVES 4 　🥄 WORK TIME 50–60 MINUTES 　🍲 COOKING TIME 25 MINUTES

EQUIPMENT

bowls

shallow dish

vegetable peeler

saucepans

chef's knife †

chopsticks

colander

small knife

dish towels

salad spinner

chopping board

strainer

rubber gloves

† cleaver can also be used

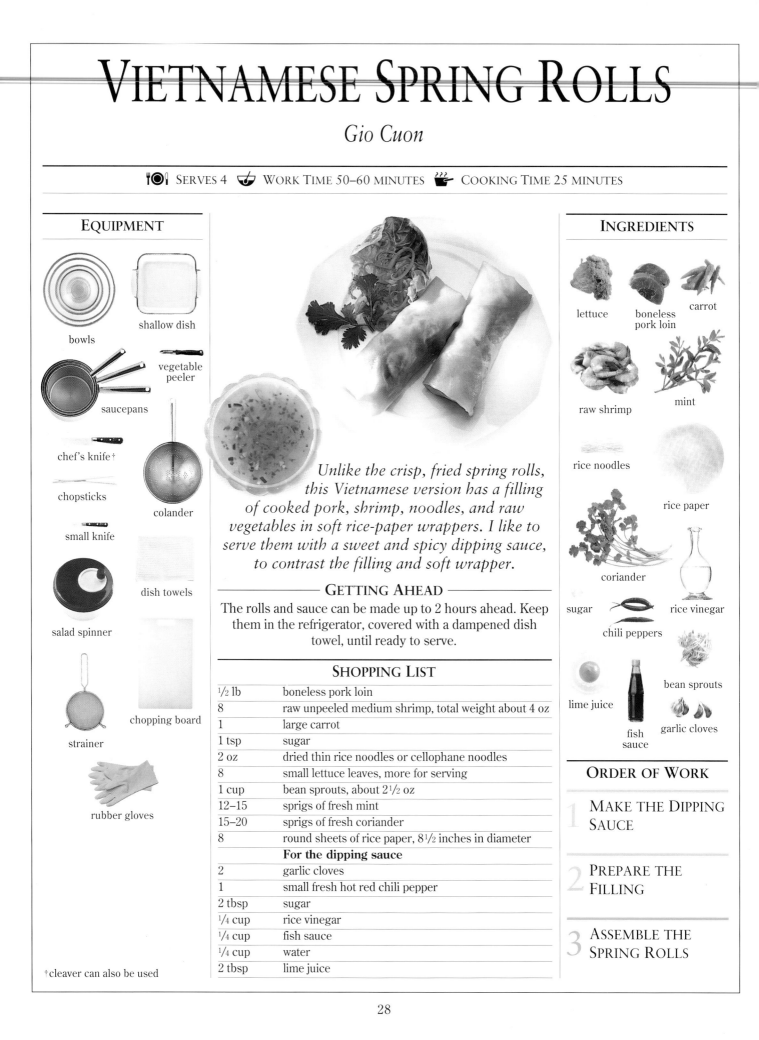

Unlike the crisp, fried spring rolls, this Vietnamese version has a filling of cooked pork, shrimp, noodles, and raw vegetables in soft rice-paper wrappers. I like to serve them with a sweet and spicy dipping sauce, to contrast the filling and soft wrapper.

GETTING AHEAD

The rolls and sauce can be made up to 2 hours ahead. Keep them in the refrigerator, covered with a dampened dish towel, until ready to serve.

SHOPPING LIST

1/2 lb	boneless pork loin
8	raw unpeeled medium shrimp, total weight about 4 oz
1	large carrot
1 tsp	sugar
2 oz	dried thin rice noodles or cellophane noodles
8	small lettuce leaves, more for serving
1 cup	bean sprouts, about 2 1/2 oz
12–15	sprigs of fresh mint
15–20	sprigs of fresh coriander
8	round sheets of rice paper, 8 1/2 inches in diameter
	For the dipping sauce
2	garlic cloves
1	small fresh hot red chili pepper
2 tbsp	sugar
1/4 cup	rice vinegar
1/4 cup	fish sauce
1/4 cup	water
2 tbsp	lime juice

INGREDIENTS

lettuce

boneless pork loin

carrot

raw shrimp

mint

rice noodles

rice paper

coriander

sugar

rice vinegar

chili peppers

lime juice

fish sauce

bean sprouts

garlic cloves

ORDER OF WORK

1 MAKE THE DIPPING SAUCE

2 PREPARE THE FILLING

3 ASSEMBLE THE SPRING ROLLS

MAKE THE DIPPING SAUCE

1 Set the flat side of the chef's knife on top of each garlic clove and strike it with your fist. Discard the skin and finely chop the garlic.

2 Wearing rubber gloves, cut the chili pepper lengthwise in half and discard the core. Scrape out the seeds and fleshy white ribs from each half.

3 Cut each chili pepper half lengthwise into very thin strips. Gather the strips together and cut across into very fine dice.

! TAKE CARE !

Be sure to wear rubber gloves when preparing fresh chili peppers, and avoid contact with your eyes because the chili peppers can burn your skin.

4 In a small bowl, combine the chopped garlic, diced chili pepper, sugar, rice vinegar, fish sauce, and water. Pour in the lime juice, and stir with the chopsticks until the sauce is thoroughly mixed.

PREPARE THE FILLING

Simmering shrimp in shell gives more flavor

Shrimp are done when shell and flesh turn pink

1 Half-fill a small saucepan with water and bring to a boil. Add the pork and simmer just until tender, 15–20 minutes.

2 Meanwhile, half-fill a medium pan with water and bring to a boil. Add the shrimp and simmer just until they turn pink, 1–2 minutes. Drain, rinse with cold water, and drain again.

HOW TO CUT JULIENNE STRIPS OF CARROT

Julienne strips of carrot make a colorful salad or garnish and are thin enough to soften in a marinade without cooking.

1 Peel and trim the carrot, and cut into pieces about 3 inches long. Square off the rounded sides of each piece of carrot.

2 Holding the carrot steady with one hand, cut it lengthwise into thin vertical slices.

3 Stack the slices, and cut lengthwise into fine strips. Keep the tip of the knife on the chopping board as you slice and guide it with your curled fingers.

3 With your fingertips, carefully peel off the shells from the shrimp, including the tail sections. Discard the shrimp shells.

Shrimp shells come off easily in your fingers

4 Cut each shrimp lengthwise in half. Using the tip of the small knife, remove the dark intestinal vein.

5 Drain the pork, rinse with cold water to remove any scum, and drain again thoroughly. When the pork is cool enough to handle, cut it horizontally in half and then cut across the grain into 1/8-inch slices.

Hold chopsticks firmly in your hand while stirring

6 Peel the carrot and trim the ends. Cut the carrot into julienne strips (see box, left). In a bowl, toss the carrot strips with the sugar, using the chopsticks, and let stand until wilted, about 15 minutes.

7 Bring a large pan of water to a boil. Add the noodles, and simmer until tender but still slightly chewy, 1–2 minutes, or according to package directions. Stir occasionally with chopsticks to prevent them from sticking.

ANNE SAYS
"If using cellophane noodles, cook them in the boiling water just until softened, about 30 seconds."

8 Drain the noodles in the strainer, rinse with cold water, and drain again thoroughly.

Drain noodles well so spring rolls do not become soggy

9 Put the noodles on the chopping board and cut them roughly into 2- to 3-inch lengths.

10 Wash the lettuce leaves in plenty of cold water and discard the tough stems. Dry the lettuce in the salad spinner or on a dish towel. Tear the large leaves into 2–3 pieces with your fingers, if necessary.

Crisp lettuce leaves add pleasant crunch to spring rolls

11 Pick over the bean sprouts, discarding any sprouts that are discolored. Remove the fine roots and green hulls from the sprouts. Strip the mint and coriander leaves from the stems with your fingers, reserving a few sprigs for garnish.

12 Reserve 2 tbsp carrot strips. Assemble the remaining filling ingredients on a large plate for easy handling.

3 ASSEMBLE THE SPRING ROLLS

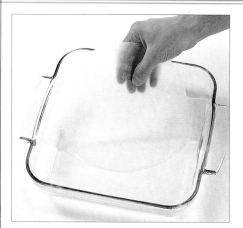

1 Pour about ½ inch of hot water into the shallow dish. Work with 1 sheet of rice paper at a time and keep the remaining sheets wrapped. Dip 1 sheet of rice paper into the water to moisten and soften it, 20–25 seconds. Remove it with your fingers, and spread it out on a dry dish towel.

Rice paper wrappers tear easily so handle carefully

3 Fold both sides of the rice paper over the enclosed filling to make a 5-inch cylinder.

4 Place a few more coriander leaves on top of the cylinder, then arrange 2 shrimp halves, cut-side down, on top of the leaves.

2 Place 1 lettuce leaf on a third of the rice paper. Top with one-eighth of the noodles, carrot, pork, bean sprouts, and mint and coriander leaves. Roll up the paper, halfway, into a cylinder.

ANNE SAYS
"Rice paper will soften as you continue to work with it, but if it seems dry, brush it lightly with a little more water."

Work quickly so rice paper remains flexible

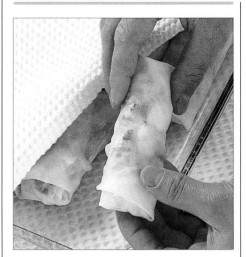

5 Continue rolling the paper into a cylinder and press the end lightly to seal. Place the roll, shrimp-side up, on a tray or plate and cover with a dampened dish towel to keep the roll moist. Repeat with the remaining rice paper and filling.

🍴 TO SERVE
Divide the sauce among 4 small bowls and sprinkle each with some of the reserved carrot julienne. Arrange 2 spring rolls on each plate. Garnish with the reserved herbs and carrot, and more lettuce if you like.

Shrimp show clearly through translucent wrapping of rice paper

VEGETARIAN SPRING ROLLS
GIO CHEY

Mushrooms and onions replace the meat in these spring rolls, which are filled with a salad of noodles, vegetables, and refreshing aromatic herbs.

1 Omit the pork, shrimp, and dipping sauce. Soak 8 dried Chinese black mushrooms in about ¾ cup boiling water until plump and softened, about 15 minutes. Meanwhile, prepare the noodles and carrots as directed. Drain the mushrooms, reserving ½ cup liquid. Squeeze the mushrooms to remove moisture. Cut off the stems. Cut the caps across into ½-inch slices.
2 Peel 1 onion, leaving a little of the root attached, cut it lengthwise in half, and cut across into thin slices.

3 Heat a wok over medium-high heat until hot, and drizzle in 1 tbsp oil to coat the bottom and sides. Continue heating until the oil is hot, add the onion, and cook, stirring, until softened, about 2 minutes. Add the mushrooms and reserved liquid. Cover and cook, stirring occasionally, until the mushrooms are tender, 3–5 minutes. Uncover and continue to cook until all liquid has evaporated. Stir in 1 tsp soy sauce, ½ tsp sugar, and salt to taste. Transfer to a bowl and let cool.
4 Assemble the spring rolls as directed, using all the carrots and replacing the shrimp with the mushroom mixture. Cover and keep cool until ready to serve.
5 Make a hoisin dipping sauce: finely chop 1 garlic clove. In a small pan, heat 2 tsp oil until hot, add the garlic and cook until fragrant, about 15 seconds. Stir in ½ cup hoisin sauce, 3 tbsp water, 1 tbsp light soy sauce, and ½ tsp dried hot red pepper flakes. Remove from the heat and let cool.
6 Pour the sauce into 4 small bowls and sprinkle with 2 tbsp chopped peanuts. Arrange 2 spring rolls on each plate, with a salad of carrot julienne, lettuce, bean sprouts, fresh herbs, and chopped peanuts, if you like.

VINEGARED RICE ROLLED IN SEAWEED

Nori-Maki

🍽 SERVES 12 🥄 WORK TIME 50–60 MINUTES* ☕ COOKING TIME 12 MINUTES

EQUIPMENT

wooden bowl

bamboo mat †

cardboard

bowls

saucepans, 1 with lid

chef's knife

chopsticks

chopping board

scissors

strainer

dish towel

wooden rice paddle ‡

† aluminum foil can also be used

‡ flat wooden spoon or spatula can also be used

INGREDIENTS

roasted seaweed

fresh raw tuna

English cucumber †

sugar   rice vinegar

Japanese horseradish powder

short-grain white rice

† Japanese or regular cucumber can also be used

ANNE SAYS

"Raw fish, essential in nori-maki, must be absolutely fresh. Purchase it from a reputable fish market and use it the same day."

ORDER OF WORK

1 PREPARE THE VINEGARED RICE

2 PREPARE THE FILLING AND ASSEMBLE THE ROLLS

3 CUT AND SERVE THE *NORI-MAKI*

The Japanese term "sushi" covers a wide assortment of vinegared rice dishes. In nori-maki, a bamboo mat is used to roll sheets of roasted seaweed, called nori, *around a filling, which is then cut into thick slices. In this recipe, half have a cucumber filling, half are rolled around strips of raw tuna.*

* *plus 30 minutes standing time*

SHOPPING LIST

	pink pickled ginger and Japanese soy sauce for serving
	cucumber fences (see page 123) for decoration (optional)
	For the vinegared rice
2¼ cups	short-grain white rice
2½ cups	water
⅓ cup	rice vinegar (preferably Japanese), more if needed
2 tbsp	sugar, more if needed
1 tsp	salt, more if needed
	For the rolls
4 tsp	Japanese horseradish powder
1 tbsp	water, more if needed
8-inch	piece of English cucumber
4 oz	fresh raw boneless tuna
6	sheets of roasted seaweed

1 PREPARE THE VINEGARED RICE

1 Put the rice in a large bowl, cover with cold water, and stir with your fingertips until the water is milky-white. Pour off the water. Repeat once or twice until the water is fairly clear.

2 Drain the rice in the strainer, then put it in a saucepan. Add the measured water, cover, and bring to a boil over high heat.

Lift lid quickly to check when water comes to a boil

3 Reduce the heat to low and simmer until the water is absorbed and the rice is tender, about 12 minutes. Remove the saucepan from the heat, and let the rice stand, without lifting the lid, about 30 minutes.

4 Meanwhile, in a small saucepan, combine the rice vinegar, sugar, and salt. Bring to a boil, stirring until the sugar dissolves. Remove from the heat and let cool.

5 Turn the hot cooked rice into the wooden bowl. Dampen the wooden paddle with water. Drizzle the vinegar and sugar mixture evenly over the rice. Immediately mix the rice and vinegar mixture together gently but thoroughly with the wooden paddle.

6 Quickly cool the rice to room temperature by fanning it with the cardboard while tossing the rice with the paddle. Add more vinegar, sugar, or salt if needed. Cover the vinegared rice with the dampened dish towel.

ANNE SAYS
"Cooling rice by fanning and tossing makes it glossy, but be careful not to crush the grains."

2 PREPARE THE FILLING AND ASSEMBLE THE ROLLS

Japanese horseradish paste adds bite to *sushi* rolls

1 Put the horseradish powder in a small bowl. With the chopsticks, mix in the water to make a thick spreadable paste.

2 Halve the piece of cucumber lengthwise. Set one half cut-side down; cut it lengthwise into 6 strips. If necessary, trim the strips to the width of the roasted seaweed sheets. Reserve the other cucumber half for the decoration, if you like.

ANNE SAYS
"*English and Japanese cucumbers have only a few tiny seeds. If using a regular cucumber, scoop out the seeds.*"

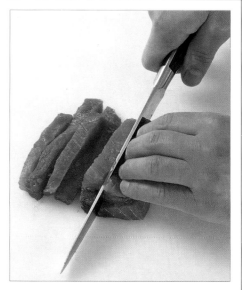

3 Rinse the tuna under cold running water, and pat dry with paper towels. Set the tuna on the chopping board and cut it into ³/₈-inch slices with the chef's knife. Stack the slices and cut into ³/₈-inch strips.

ANNE SAYS
"*The tuna will be easier to slice if it is partially frozen or well-chilled.*"

4 Pour some water into a small bowl for moistening your fingers. Cut each sheet of seaweed crosswise in half with the scissors. Lay 1 piece, smooth-side down, on the bamboo mat, placing it so the long edges are parallel to the lines of the mat.

Nori sheets are stiff but flexible

5 Moisten your fingers lightly with water, then spread about ¹/₂ cup of the cooked rice in an even ¹/₄-inch layer on the piece of seaweed, leaving a ¹/₂-inch strip uncovered at the end furthest away from you.

6 Spread a thin line of horseradish paste lengthwise along the center of the rice with your finger.

Horseradish paste makes *nori-maki* slightly spicy

7 Make 6 cucumber *sushi* rolls: arrange 1 of the cucumber strips lengthwise along the middle over the line of horseradish paste on the layer of vinegared rice.

8 Starting from the edge closest to you, lift the mat and seaweed securely together and fold it away from you over the filling. Press down firmly and roll up the seaweed, lifting the mat at the same time.

9 Once you have reached the exposed end of the seaweed, moisten it lightly with wet fingertips to seal the roll.

Pulling on bamboo mat helps tighten roll

10 Wrap and press the mat around the roll to shape it into a smooth tight cylinder. Unroll the mat and transfer the cucumber roll to the chopping board. Repeat to make 5 more cucumber rolls.

11 Make 6 tuna *sushi* rolls in the same way as the cucumber rolls, piecing the tuna strips together as necessary to cover the full length of the seaweed and rice.

3 CUT AND SERVE THE *NORI-MAKI*

Cut cleanly through *nori-maki* with very sharp knife

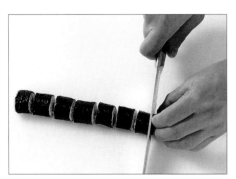

1 Moisten the chef's knife with a damp dish towel. Cut 1 cucumber roll crosswise into 3 equal pieces. Wipe the knife clean between cuts with the damp towel.

2 Cut each piece of cucumber roll crosswise in half at a slight angle. Repeat with the remaining rolls.

3 Cut each tuna roll crosswise into 8 equal pieces, wiping the knife with the damp cloth between cuts.

Pink pickled ginger is formed into flower shapes and eaten with the rolls

Japanese soy sauce is the classic accompaniment to *nori-maki*

¶◉¶ TO SERVE

Divide the pieces of tuna and cucumber *nori-maki* among 12 individual serving plates, setting them cut- and angled-side up. Decorate each plate with pickled ginger (curling the pieces into flower shapes), and cucumber fences, if you like. Serve with Japanese soy sauce for dipping.

GETTING AHEAD

The rice can be cooked and vinegared up to 4 hours ahead and kept, covered with a damp dish towel. The *nori-maki* can be rolled up to 2 hours ahead and refrigerated; slice them just before serving.

VARIATION
RICE MOUNDS TOPPED WITH SHRIMP
NIGIRI-SUSHI

In sushi bars, rice mounds are topped with a variety of sliced fish, shrimp, and cooked eggs. They are usually eaten with the fingers. Each piece is turned over so that the topping is underneath and dipped into soy sauce before eating.

1 Omit the roasted seaweed, cucumber, and tuna. Prepare the vinegared rice as directed, using 1 cup rice and 1 cup plus 2 tbsp water. For the vinegar mixture, use 3 tbsp vinegar, 1 tbsp sugar, and 1/4 tsp salt.
2 Prepare the horseradish paste as directed, using 2 tsp horseradish powder and 1 1/2 tsp water.
3 Peel the shells from 16–18 raw large shrimp (total weight about 1 lb), leaving the last tail section attached. Insert a wooden toothpick lengthwise through each shrimp to prevent it from curling when cooked.
4 Half-fill a saucepan with water; bring to a boil. Add 1 tsp rice vinegar and 1/4 tsp salt. Add the shrimp and simmer just until they turn pink, 1–2 minutes. Drain, and rinse with cold water.

5 Set the shrimp, front-side up, on the chopping board. With a small knife, make a deep incision along the underside to the toothpick, then remove it. Continue cutting so the shrimp opens like a butterfly and remove the dark intestinal vein.

! TAKE CARE !
Do not cut the shrimp too deeply or they will separate into 2 pieces. You will also have to cut through the shell in the last tail section to flatten out the shrimp.

6 With moistened hands, divide the vinegared rice into the same number of portions as you have shrimp. Hold 1 portion of rice in the palm of your hand and press it with the fingers of your other hand

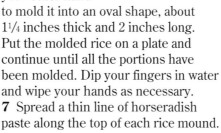

to mold it into an oval shape, about 1 1/4 inches thick and 2 inches long. Put the molded rice on a plate and continue until all the portions have been molded. Dip your fingers in water and wipe your hands as necessary.
7 Spread a thin line of horseradish paste along the top of each rice mound.

8 Press a butterflied shrimp, cut-side down, firmly on top of the rice mound.
9 Arrange on a serving plate and spread the tail section flat. Decorate with cucumber fences, cucumber julienne, and pickled ginger, if you like. Serve with Japanese soy sauce for dipping. Serves 8.

THAI SKEWERED CHICKEN

Gai Satay

🍴 SERVES 4 🥣 WORK TIME 20–30 MINUTES* 🍲 COOKING TIME 6–8 MINUTES

EQUIPMENT

bowls

boning knife †

chef's knife †

chopsticks

twelve 8-inch bamboo skewers

chopping board

† cleaver can also be used

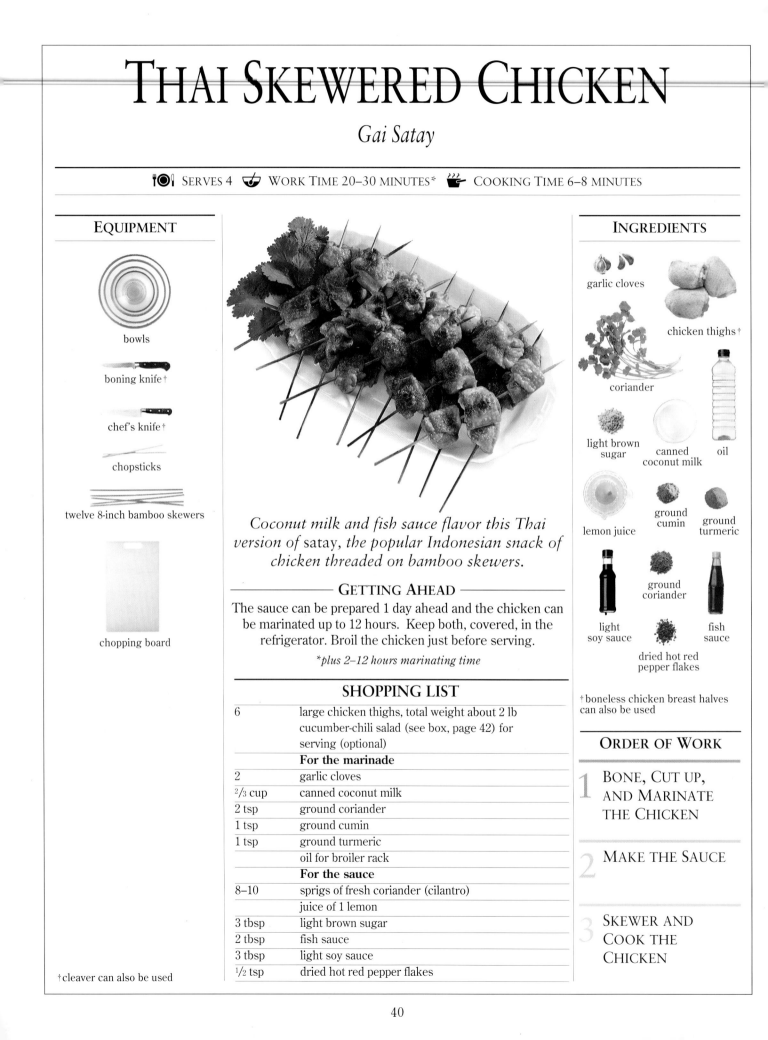

Coconut milk and fish sauce flavor this Thai version of satay, *the popular Indonesian snack of chicken threaded on bamboo skewers.*

GETTING AHEAD

The sauce can be prepared 1 day ahead and the chicken can be marinated up to 12 hours. Keep both, covered, in the refrigerator. Broil the chicken just before serving.

*plus 2–12 hours marinating time

SHOPPING LIST

6	large chicken thighs, total weight about 2 lb
	cucumber-chili salad (see box, page 42) for serving (optional)
	For the marinade
2	garlic cloves
²/₃ cup	canned coconut milk
2 tsp	ground coriander
1 tsp	ground cumin
1 tsp	ground turmeric
	oil for broiler rack
	For the sauce
8–10	sprigs of fresh coriander (cilantro)
	juice of 1 lemon
3 tbsp	light brown sugar
2 tbsp	fish sauce
3 tbsp	light soy sauce
½ tsp	dried hot red pepper flakes

INGREDIENTS

garlic cloves

chicken thighs †

coriander

light brown sugar

canned coconut milk

oil

lemon juice

ground cumin

ground turmeric

ground coriander

light soy sauce

dried hot red pepper flakes

fish sauce

† boneless chicken breast halves can also be used

ORDER OF WORK

1 BONE, CUT UP, AND MARINATE THE CHICKEN

2 MAKE THE SAUCE

3 SKEWER AND COOK THE CHICKEN

1 BONE, CUT UP, AND MARINATE THE CHICKEN

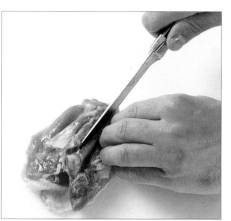

1 With the boning knife, make a deep slit on the underside of each chicken thigh, along the bone.

2 Free the meat at 1 end of the bone, then scrape the meat off the bone until you reach the other end. Cut the meat free from the bone.

Cut boned thighs into even pieces

3 Set the meat on the chopping board; cut each thigh into 6 even chunks, discarding any fat and sinew.

Hold skin taut to make cutting easier

4 Make the marinade: set the flat side of the chef's knife on each garlic clove and strike it with your fist. Discard the skin and chop the garlic.

5 Combine the garlic, coconut milk, coriander, cumin, and turmeric in a large bowl, and mix well with the chopsticks.

6 Add the chunks of chicken and toss until well coated with the marinade. Cover the bowl and set aside to marinate, at least 2 hours and up to 12 hours.

ANNE SAYS
"If marinating the chicken for more than 2 hours, cover, and refrigerate it."

Stir the marinade from time to time to keep the pieces coated

2 MAKE THE SAUCE

1 Strip the coriander leaves from the stems. Reserve a few leaves for decoration. Pile the remainder on the chopping board and coarsely chop them.

2 In a small bowl, combine the lemon juice, brown sugar, fish sauce, soy sauce, red pepper flakes, and chopped coriander and stir until mixed. Cover the bowl and refrigerate the sauce until ready to serve.

Chopsticks are excellent for stirring

CUCUMBER-CHILI SALAD

This simple salad is delicious when served with either broiled or grilled dishes. The longer the salad is left to marinate, the hotter and spicier it will be.

🍽 SERVES 4

🥢 WORK TIME 15–20 MINUTES*

* plus at least 1 hour marinating time

SHOPPING LIST

½ cup	water
½ cup	sugar
½ tsp	salt
½ cup	rice vinegar
1	large cucumber
1	fresh hot red chili pepper

For less heat, use only half a chili pepper

1 Combine the water, sugar, and salt in a small saucepan. Bring to a boil, stirring with chopsticks, until the sugar dissolves. Remove from the heat, stir in the vinegar, and let cool.

2 Peel and trim the cucumber. Cut it lengthwise in half, and scoop out the seeds with a teaspoon. Cut the halves crosswise into thin slices.

3 Wearing rubber gloves, cut the chili pepper lengthwise in half, discarding the core. Scrape out the seeds and cut away the fleshy white ribs from each half. Cut each half lengthwise into very thin strips.

4 Combine the cucumber, chili pepper, and vinegar mixture in a bowl. Cover, and marinate in the refrigerator, at least 1 hour and up to 4 hours. Taste just before serving.

3 SKEWER AND COOK THE CHICKEN

1 Put the bamboo skewers in a dish of cold water to soak (so they do not burn during broiling), 30 minutes. Drain. Heat the broiler and lightly oil the broiler rack. Thread the chicken chunks, skin-side up, onto the skewers, dividing them equally.

2 Arrange the skewers, skin-side up, on the oiled rack. Broil about 3 inches from the heat until speckled with brown, 4–5 minutes. Turn the skewers and continue broiling until the chicken is no longer pink in the center, 2–3 minutes longer. (Broil in batches if necessary to avoid crowding.)

🍴 TO SERVE
Arrange the chicken skewers on a warmed serving platter, decorate with the reserved coriander leaves, and serve with the sauce. Pass the salad separately, if using.

Sauce is lively with sweet, sour, and hot flavors

Chicken broils to a golden brown

VARIATION

JAPANESE CHICKEN KEBABS
YAKITORI

A typical Japanese meal includes at least one grilled dish, either fish or chicken. A charcoal grill is ideal, but a broiler or stove-top grill works well.

1 Omit the marinade and the sauce. Prepare the chicken thighs as directed.
2 Make a sweet soy sauce: combine 1/2 cup Japanese soy sauce, 1/4 cup Japanese rice wine, and 3 tbsp sugar in a saucepan. Bring to a boil, stirring to dissolve the sugar; set aside.
3 Prepare the salad as directed, omitting the chili pepper. Soak the skewers as directed.
4 Trim 6 scallions and cut into 1 1/2-inch lengths. Thread the chicken, skin-side up, and scallions alternately onto skewers, beginning and ending with chicken.
5 Broil the kebabs, skin-side up, about 2 minutes, then brush with the sweet soy sauce. Continue broiling, turning once, brushing frequently with sauce, until the chicken is glazed and no longer pink in the center, about 3 minutes on each side.
6 Skim the fat from the broiler pan and add the juices to the remaining sauce in the saucepan. Bring to a boil, and pour into small serving bowls. Arrange the kebabs on warmed plates, and serve with the sauce and cucumber salad.

STEAMED FISH IN BLACK BEAN SAUCE

Zang Yu Dau Shi

🍽 SERVES 4   ⏲ WORK TIME 20–25 MINUTES*   ♨ COOKING TIME 12–15 MINUTES

EQUIPMENT

bowls

small bamboo steamer †

wok

strainer

paper towels

cleaver ‡

chopping board

chopsticks

Blessed with miles of coastline, Chinese cooks prepare fish, preferably whole, in innumerable ways. This fish dish is steamed, one of the classic Chinese cooking methods, and seasoned with fermented black beans, garlic, ginger, and soy. With steaming, the fish retains its moisture and flavor.

GETTING AHEAD

The fish, seasoning, and decoration can be prepared up to 4 hours ahead and kept separately, covered, in the refrigerator. Do not steam the fish until ready to serve.

*plus 30 minutes soaking time

SHOPPING LIST

4	scallions
1	whole red snapper, cleaned and scaled, weighing about 2 lb
1 tbsp	Chinese rice wine
4	garlic cloves
3 tbsp	fermented black beans
2-inch	piece of fresh ginger root
2 tbsp	light soy sauce
1 tbsp	dark sesame oil
1/2 tsp	sugar

INGREDIENTS

red snapper †

fresh ginger root

fermented black beans

light soy sauce

scallions

garlic cloves

sugar

Chinese rice wine ‡

dark sesame oil

† other firm-fleshed fish, such as sea bass, bream, or carp can also be used

‡ dry sherry can also be used

ANNE SAYS
"Ask your fish store to clean and scale the fish for you."

ORDER OF WORK

1 PREPARE THE DECORATION, THE FISH, AND THE BLACK BEAN SAUCE

2 STEAM THE FISH

† round rack can also be used
‡ chef's knife can also be used

PREPARE THE DECORATION, THE FISH, AND THE BLACK BEAN SAUCE

1 Make the scallion brushes (see box, page 46), reserving the green tops. Cut the tops lengthwise into thin julienne strips. Reserve for decoration.

2 Rinse the fish and pat dry with paper towels. Using the cleaver, slash the flesh diagonally to the bone, 3 times on each side, at 1-inch intervals.

ANNE SAYS
"The fish is slashed to prevent the skin from bursting during cooking and to allow the heat and flavorings to penetrate."

Chinese rice wine is amber in color and slightly sweet

3 Rub the fish, including inside the slashes, with the rice wine. Set the fish on an oval heatproof platter.

4 Set the flat side of the cleaver on top of each garlic clove and strike it with your fist. Discard the skin and finely chop the garlic.

5 Put the black beans in the strainer, rinse with cold water to remove any excess salt, and drain thoroughly. Coarsely chop the beans.

Ginger is crushed and chopped to extract maximum flavor for sauce

6 Scrape the skin from the ginger root. Slice the ginger, cutting across the fibrous grain. Crush half of the slices with the flat of the cleaver, then finely chop them. Stack the remaining slices and cut into thin strips.

HOW TO MAKE SCALLION BRUSHES

Scallion brushes are an easy and effective decoration for many Asian dishes.

1 Trim the scallions, leaving a little of the green tops. Cut the scallions across into 3-inch lengths.

2 With the tip of the cleaver blade, make several slashes about 1-inch deep at both ends of each scallion piece. Spread the ends gently to open the slashes.

3 Put the scallions in a bowl of ice water and chill until the ends have curled, about 30 minutes.

Fermented black beans are boiled and soaked in brine

7 Combine the garlic, black beans, finely chopped ginger, soy sauce, sesame oil, and sugar in a bowl, and stir well to mix.

STEAM THE FISH

Bamboo steamer sits firmly in base of wok

1 Place the small bamboo steamer in the wok. Add enough water to come halfway up the side of the steamer. Cover the wok and bring the water to a boil over high heat.

ANNE SAYS
"Be sure that the steamer will hold the platter with the fish securely, without it touching the sides of the wok. The steam must be able to circulate freely."

8 Spread about half of the black bean mixture on one side of the fish. Turn the fish over and spread the remaining mixture over the fish. Sprinkle the strips of fresh ginger in an even layer on the fish.

! TAKE CARE !
If using a round-bottomed wok, place it on a wok ring for added stability when steaming.

2 Uncover the wok and place the platter with the fish on the steamer over the boiling water. Cover tightly and reduce the heat to medium-high.

3 Steam the fish over the water until the flesh is opaque and flakes easily when tested with chopsticks, 12–15 minutes.

4 Carefully remove the platter from the wok. Spoon some of the black bean sauce from the platter over the fish. Sprinkle the green scallion strips on top.

🍴 **TO SERVE**
Drain the scallion brushes thoroughly and add them as decoration to the platter.

Whole red snapper, steamed Chinese-style, makes a colorful presentation

Crisp slices of scallion refresh pungent black bean sauce

VARIATION

LEMON GRASS AND BASIL SCENTED STEAMED FISH

Thai-inspired flavorings of lemon grass and basil replace the black bean sauce in this light and fragrant dish.

1 Omit the scallion brushes and strips, fermented black beans, sesame oil, and sugar. Prepare the fish as directed.
2 Prepare the garlic and ginger root as directed. Combine the garlic and chopped ginger with the soy sauce, 3 tbsp fish sauce, 1 tsp brown sugar, and $1/2$ tsp freshly ground black pepper.
3 Cut off the dry leafy tops from 2 stalks of lemon grass, leaving 5–6 inches of stalk. Peel away any dry outer layers until you reach the tender core. Crush the lemon grass stalks with the flat of the cleaver, then cut them crosswise into 2-inch pieces.
4 Tuck the lemon grass and 4 basil sprigs inside the fish cavity. Arrange the fish on a platter. Spoon about one-third of the garlic mixture inside the cavity and the remainder on both sides of the fish. Add the ginger strips, and steam as directed. Serve as directed, decorated with more basil sprigs, if you like.

SPICED SEAFOOD SALAD

Yum Pla Talay

🍴 SERVES 4 🥣 WORK TIME 30–40 MINUTES 🍲 COOKING TIME 12–15 MINUTES

EQUIPMENT

bowls

paper towels

large saucepan

bamboo skimmer †

rubber gloves

citrus juicer

chef's knife ‡

small knife

small strainer

chopsticks

chopping board

† slotted spoon can also be used
‡ cleaver can also be used

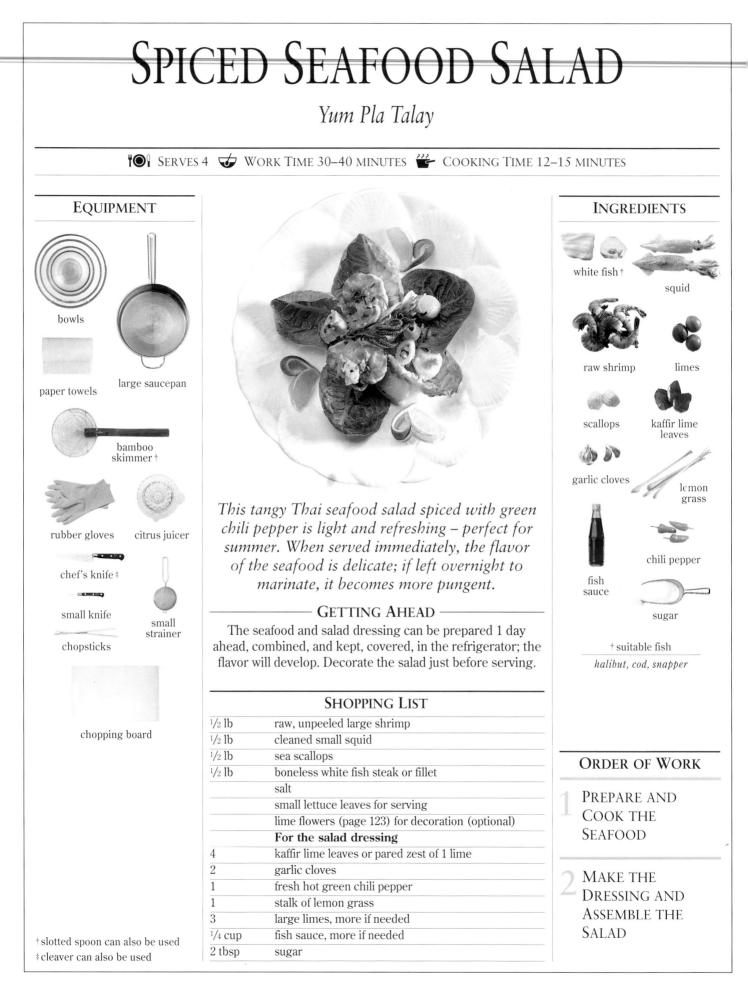

This tangy Thai seafood salad spiced with green chili pepper is light and refreshing – perfect for summer. When served immediately, the flavor of the seafood is delicate; if left overnight to marinate, it becomes more pungent.

GETTING AHEAD

The seafood and salad dressing can be prepared 1 day ahead, combined, and kept, covered, in the refrigerator; the flavor will develop. Decorate the salad just before serving.

SHOPPING LIST

¹/₂ lb	raw, unpeeled large shrimp
¹/₂ lb	cleaned small squid
¹/₂ lb	sea scallops
¹/₂ lb	boneless white fish steak or fillet
	salt
	small lettuce leaves for serving
	lime flowers (page 123) for decoration (optional)
	For the salad dressing
4	kaffir lime leaves or pared zest of 1 lime
2	garlic cloves
1	fresh hot green chili pepper
1	stalk of lemon grass
3	large limes, more if needed
¹/₄ cup	fish sauce, more if needed
2 tbsp	sugar

INGREDIENTS

white fish †

squid

raw shrimp

limes

scallops

kaffir lime leaves

garlic cloves

lemon grass

chili pepper

fish sauce

sugar

† suitable fish

halibut, cod, snapper

ORDER OF WORK

1 **PREPARE AND COOK THE SEAFOOD**

2 **MAKE THE DRESSING AND ASSEMBLE THE SALAD**

1 PREPARE AND COOK THE SEAFOOD

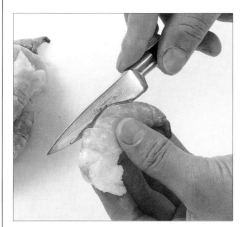

1 Peel off the shells from the shrimp with your fingers. Make a shallow cut along the back of each shrimp with the small knife and remove the dark intestinal vein. Rinse the shrimp and pat dry with paper towels.

Squid is easy to prepare when already cleaned at fish store

2 Rinse the squid with cold water and pat dry with paper towels. Cut the bodies crosswise into ½-inch-wide rings. Cut the tentacles into 2–3 pieces if large.

3 If necessary, pull off and discard the small white muscle at the side of each scallop. Rinse the scallops with cold water and drain on paper towels. Cut large scallops into 2 rounds.

4 Rinse the white fish with cold running water and pat dry with paper towels.

5 Line a tray with paper towels. Fill the large saucepan with 2 inches of water, add a pinch of salt, and bring to a boil. Reduce the heat, add the squid, and simmer until the pieces are opaque and start to curl, about 2 minutes. Remove the squid with the bamboo skimmer and drain on the paper towels.

Shrimp only require brief cooking so they do not become rubbery

6 Add the shrimp to the simmering water and cook until they just turn pink, 1–2 minutes. With the bamboo skimmer, remove the shrimp and drain on the paper towels with the squid.

7 Add the white fish to the simmering water and cook until firm, about 2 minutes. Remove with the skimmer and drain on the paper towels with the squid and shrimp.

8 Add the scallops to the simmering water and cook until opaque, 1–2 minutes. Drain with the skimmer and add to the remaining seafood.

ANNE SAYS
"Cooking the seafood just at a simmer keeps it tender."

White fish skin may be removed after cooking

Squid tentacles add interesting feature to salad

2 MAKE THE DRESSING AND ASSEMBLE THE SALAD

1 Cut out any hard central veins from the lime leaves, if necessary. Stack the leaves (or lime zest), and cut lengthwise into ⅛-inch strips. Gather the strips together and cut across into very fine dice.

2 Set the flat side of the chef's knife on top of each garlic clove and strike it with your fist. Discard the skin and finely chop the garlic.

3 Wearing rubber gloves, cut the chili pepper lengthwise in half; discard the core. Scrape out the seeds and cut away the white ribs. Cut each half into very thin strips, gather together, and cut into very fine dice.

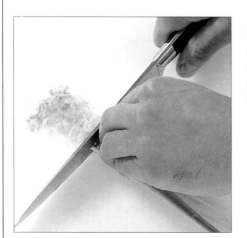

4 Cut the dry leafy top from the stalk of lemon grass. Peel away any dry outer layers until you reach the moist, tender core. Crush the lemon grass stalk with the flat of the chef's knife, then cut it crosswise into thin slices.

5 Halve the limes, squeeze the juice, and strain it. There should be about ⅓ cup juice.

6 Put the lime leaves, garlic, chili pepper, lemon grass, lime juice, fish sauce, and sugar in a small bowl. Stir until the sugar dissolves.

7 Put the shrimp, squid, and scallops in a large bowl. Pour the dressing over the seafood. Toss the mixture to coat the seafood thoroughly.

8 Remove the skin from the white fish, if necessary, then add the fish to the seafood mixture. Toss gently to break up the fish into large pieces. Taste for seasoning, adding more lime juice or fish sauce if necessary.

🍴 TO SERVE
Arrange a bed of lettuce leaves on individual plates, then mound the seafood on top. Decorate with the lime flowers, if you like.

Decorative flowers made from lime wedges can be squeezed for extra flavor

Lettuce leaves form crisp base for spicy salad

VARIATION
SPICED SEAFOOD AND CHILLED NOODLE SALAD
In this refreshing salad, shellfish and squid are stir-fried, tossed in dressing, and served chilled on a bed of dressed rice noodles.

1 Omit the white fish and lettuce leaves. Prepare the shrimp, squid, and scallops as directed.
2 Heat a wok over high heat until hot and drizzle in 2 tsp oil to coat the bottom and sides. Continue heating until the oil is hot, then add the shrimp, and stir-fry, about 30 seconds. Add the squid and scallops; stir-fry, tossing gently until the ingredients just lose their transparency (shrimp should be pink), 1½–2 minutes longer. Transfer the seafood to a bowl and set aside.
3 Prepare the salad dressing as directed and pour two-thirds over the warm seafood. Toss the seafood gently, cover, and chill, at least 2 hours and up to 24 hours. Cover and chill the remaining dressing.
4 Bring a large saucepan of water to a boil. Add 6 oz thin rice noodles and simmer them until they are tender but still slightly chewy, 1–2 minutes, or according to package directions. Drain the noodles in a colander, rinse with cold water until completely cool, then drain again thoroughly. Toss the noodles with the remaining dressing and 2 tbsp sesame oil until evenly coated. Chill, at least 1 hour.
5 To serve, arrange a bed of cold dressed noodles in individual bowls and top with the seafood. Decorate with lime wedges, if you like.

JAPANESE ONE-POT MEAL

Yosenabe

🍴 SERVES 4   🥣 WORK TIME 40–50 MINUTES*   🍲 COOKING TIME 5–7 MINUTES

EQUIPMENT

cheesecloth

vegetable peeler

Japanese earthenware pot and table-top burner

saucepans

strainer

chef's knife

chopsticks

bowls

colander

dish towel†

oyster knife

paper towels

small knife

small stiff brush

†salad spinner can also be used

ANNE SAYS
"*The traditional Japanese cooking vessel for this dish is a* donabe, *a ceramic pot with sloping sides and a domed lid, which is placed on a table-top burner. An attractive flameproof earthenware casserole can also be used.*"

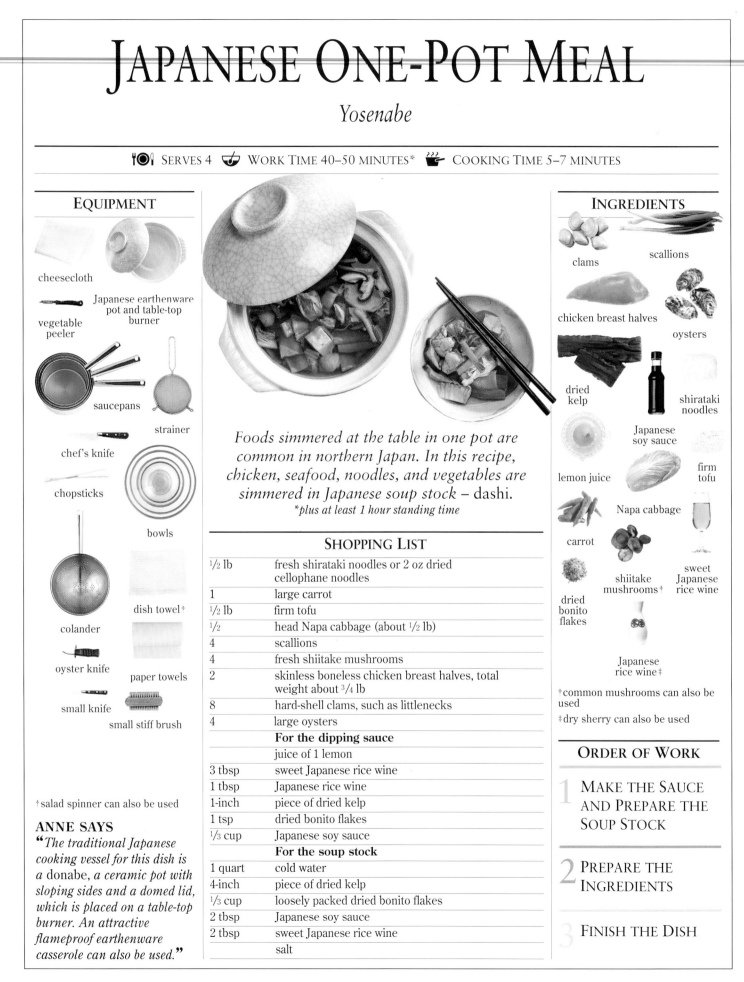

Foods simmered at the table in one pot are common in northern Japan. In this recipe, chicken, seafood, noodles, and vegetables are simmered in Japanese soup stock – dashi.
*plus at least 1 hour standing time

INGREDIENTS

clams

scallions

chicken breast halves

oysters

dried kelp

shirataki noodles

Japanese soy sauce

lemon juice

firm tofu

Napa cabbage

carrot

shiitake mushrooms†

sweet Japanese rice wine

dried bonito flakes

Japanese rice wine‡

†common mushrooms can also be used

‡dry sherry can also be used

SHOPPING LIST

½ lb	fresh shirataki noodles or 2 oz dried cellophane noodles
1	large carrot
½ lb	firm tofu
½	head Napa cabbage (about ½ lb)
4	scallions
4	fresh shiitake mushrooms
2	skinless boneless chicken breast halves, total weight about ¾ lb
8	hard-shell clams, such as littlenecks
4	large oysters
	For the dipping sauce
	juice of 1 lemon
3 tbsp	sweet Japanese rice wine
1 tbsp	Japanese rice wine
1-inch	piece of dried kelp
1 tsp	dried bonito flakes
⅓ cup	Japanese soy sauce
	For the soup stock
1 quart	cold water
4-inch	piece of dried kelp
⅓ cup	loosely packed dried bonito flakes
2 tbsp	Japanese soy sauce
2 tbsp	sweet Japanese rice wine
	salt

ORDER OF WORK

1. MAKE THE SAUCE AND PREPARE THE SOUP STOCK

2. PREPARE THE INGREDIENTS

3. FINISH THE DISH

1 MAKE THE SAUCE AND PREPARE THE SOUP STOCK

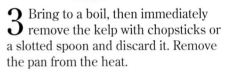

Softened kelp is removed to leave delicately flavored stock

1 For the dipping sauce, combine the lemon juice, both rice wines, dried kelp, bonito flakes, and soy sauce in a bowl. Let stand at room temperature, at least 1 hour or up to 24 hours. Meanwhile, make the soup stock.

2 For the soup stock, pour the cold water into a large saucepan, and add the 4-inch piece of dried kelp.

3 Bring to a boil, then immediately remove the kelp with chopsticks or a slotted spoon and discard it. Remove the pan from the heat.

! TAKE CARE !
Remove the kelp as soon as the water comes to a boil; if it is allowed to boil, the stock will be bitter and cloudy.

Cheesecloth catches very fine bonito flakes to give clear stock

4 Sprinkle the dried bonito flakes evenly over the surface of the kelp-infused water. Let the stock stand until the flakes settle to the bottom, 3–5 minutes, depending on the thickness and dryness of the flakes. Line the strainer with dampened cheesecloth.

5 Strain the stock through the cheesecloth into the pot. Add the soy sauce and sweet rice wine. Stir, and taste for seasoning, adding salt if necessary.

2 PREPARE THE INGREDIENTS

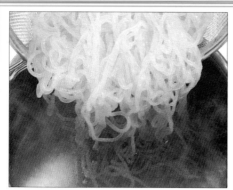

1 Bring a large saucepan of water to a boil. Drain the shirataki noodles if necessary, and add them to the pan. Boil until firm but still slightly chewy, about 1 minute, stirring them occasionally with the chopsticks.

ANNE SAYS
"If using cellophane noodles, soak them in a bowl of warm water until soft, 30 minutes, then proceed as for the shirataki noodles."

2 Drain the noodles, rinse with cold water, and drain again. On the chopping board, cut the noodles into 4- to 5-inch lengths.

Carrots are thinly sliced to cook quickly

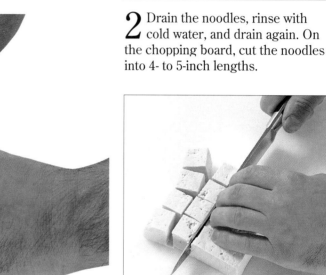

3 Peel the carrot and trim the ends. Cut the carrot into 2-inch pieces. Cut each of the pieces lengthwise into $\frac{1}{8}$-inch slices.

4 Rinse the tofu under cold water, and drain. Set it on the chopping board and cut it into 1-inch strips. Cut the strips across into 1-inch cubes.

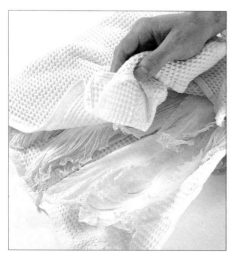

5 Trim the base from the wedge of cabbage and discard it. Separate the leaves. Wash the leaves in plenty of cold water, then dry them on the dish towel or in a salad spinner.

Napa cabbage, also called Chinese cabbage, is popular in Japan

6 Stack the leaves on top of each other, and slice across into 1-inch strips.

7 Trim the scallions and cut them across into 2-inch pieces, including some of the green tops.

8 Wipe the mushrooms with damp paper towels. Trim off and discard the woody stems. Slice the caps.

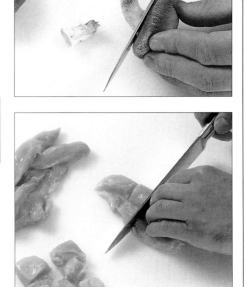

Shirataki noodles, "white waterfall" in Japanese, are made from a starchy root

9 Arrange the tofu, vegetables, and noodles on a large plate or tray. Cover tightly and chill.

Arrange tofu with vegetables for attractive presentation

10 Separate the small piece of fillet meat from each chicken breast by pulling it off with your fingers. Strip the tendon from each fillet, stroking it with the knife to remove it cleanly. Cut each breast lengthwise in half, then cut across into 1-inch pieces. Cut each fillet into 2–3 pieces. Cover, and chill.

11 Scrub and rinse the clams. With a dish towel in one hand, grip a clam, keeping the hinge of the shell between your thumb and fingers. Holding the oyster knife in your other hand, press the cutting edge of the knife between the halves opposite the hinge. Push the knife into the clam and rotate the blade to pry the shell open.

Clam is easily removed from shell with pointed knife

12 Cut the muscle from the top and bottom shells and discard the top shell. Repeat the process to open the remaining clams.

Guard on oyster knife protects your hand

13 Scrub and rinse the oysters. With a folded dish towel in one hand, grip an oyster. Holding the oyster knife in your other hand, insert the point of the blade next to the hinge of the shell. Twist to pry the shell open. Cut the top muscle of the oyster from the shell and discard the top shell.

14 Using the blade of the oyster knife, cut loose the muscle from the lower half of the shell. Repeat with the remaining oysters.

Carefully sever oyster muscle to open shell so meat remains whole

Even-sized pieces of chicken will all cook at same rate

Oyster shells are perfect vessels for presenting oysters

15 Arrange the chicken in a bowl, and the clams and oysters on the half-shell on a serving platter.

FINISH THE DISH

1 Line the strainer with clean cheesecloth. Strain the dipping sauce into a measuring cup, and pour it into 4 small bowls. Set the pot on the table-top burner. Slowly bring the stock to a boil over medium heat.

2 When the stock is simmering, add the chicken and carrot, using the chopsticks. Cook until the chicken is firm and the carrot is almost tender, 2–3 minutes.

3 Add half of the tofu, vegetables, and noodles and cook until the vegetables are tender, 2–3 minutes. Add all the oysters and clams, without their shells, and cook just until the edges of the oysters start to curl.

🍽️ TO SERVE

Guests can help themselves to the cooked ingredients, using chopsticks to dip them into the sauce before eating. When the pot is empty, replenish it with the remaining ingredients and cook until tender. When these ingredients are finished, ladle the remaining broth into bowls and serve.

Yosenabe, cooked and served in the *donabe,* is truly a one-pot meal

V A R I A T I O N
BRAISED BEEF AND VEGETABLES

SUKIYAKI
Cooked at the table in a sukiyaki nabe, or cast-iron pan, this is the most famous Japanese one-pot dish. A heavy cast-iron skillet can also be used.

1 Omit the carrot, chicken, oysters, clams, and dipping sauce. Freeze 1¼ lb boneless beef rib until firm, about 1 hour (this makes it easier to slice).

2 Prepare stock as directed, using 1 cup water, 1-inch piece of dried kelp, and 1 tbsp dried bonito. Strain stock; add ½ cup Japanese soy sauce, ¼ cup sweet Japanese rice wine, and 2 tbsp sugar.
3 Prepare the noodles, tofu, cabbage, and scallions as directed. Wipe and trim 8 fresh shiitake mushrooms. Cut a decorative cross in the top of each cap. Discard the tough stems and ribs from ¼ lb fresh Asian or regular spinach leaves, then wash the leaves thoroughly. Dry the leaves in a salad spinner or on a dish towel. Arrange the tofu, noodles, and vegetables on a tray.
4 Cut the beef across into thin slices and arrange on a tray. Cover and let the beef come to room temperature.
5 Heat 2 tbsp vegetable oil in a *sukiyaki nabe* on a table-top burner over high heat. Add half of the beef and brown lightly, stirring constantly with cooking chopsticks, 1–2 minutes. Push the meat to one side of the pan. Add half of the remaining ingredients, in separate mounds. Pour in half of the soup stock and bring to a boil. Reduce the heat to simmer the stock. Cook the meat and vegetables 2–3 minutes, stirring each ingredient to cook evenly, but keeping each mound separate.
6 Let each guest help themselves to the cooked ingredients, with chopsticks. Add the remaining ingredients to the pan as needed.

— **GETTING AHEAD** —
The sauce, stock, and remaining ingredients except the seafood, can be prepared up to 1 day ahead, and kept, covered, in the refrigerator.

LEMON GRASS CHICKEN

Ga Xao Xa Ot

🍽 SERVES 4   🥣 WORK TIME 45–55 MINUTES*   ♨ COOKING TIME ABOUT 10 MINUTES

EQUIPMENT

cleaver †

chopsticks

wok

bowls

rubber gloves

salad spinner ‡

colander

wok spatula

chopping board

pepper mill

vegetable peeler

† boning knife and chef's knife can also be used

‡ dish towel can also be used

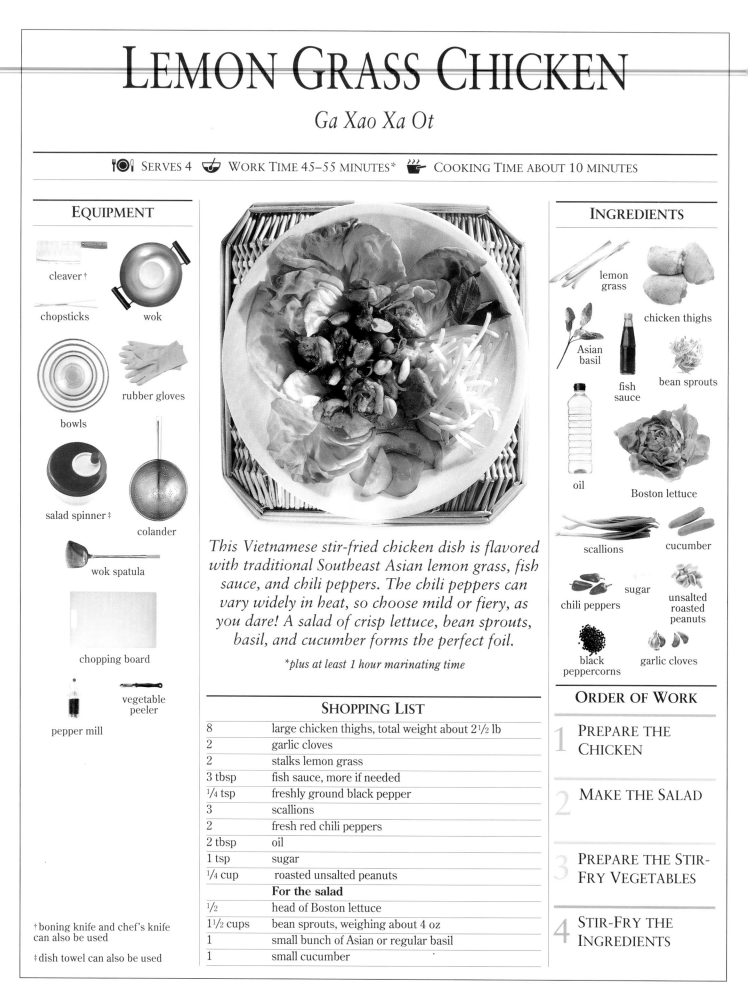

This Vietnamese stir-fried chicken dish is flavored with traditional Southeast Asian lemon grass, fish sauce, and chili peppers. The chili peppers can vary widely in heat, so choose mild or fiery, as you dare! A salad of crisp lettuce, bean sprouts, basil, and cucumber forms the perfect foil.

*plus at least 1 hour marinating time

INGREDIENTS

lemon grass

chicken thighs

Asian basil

fish sauce

bean sprouts

oil

Boston lettuce

scallions

cucumber

chili peppers

sugar

unsalted roasted peanuts

black peppercorns

garlic cloves

SHOPPING LIST

8	large chicken thighs, total weight about 2½ lb
2	garlic cloves
2	stalks lemon grass
3 tbsp	fish sauce, more if needed
¼ tsp	freshly ground black pepper
3	scallions
2	fresh red chili peppers
2 tbsp	oil
1 tsp	sugar
¼ cup	roasted unsalted peanuts
	For the salad
½	head of Boston lettuce
1½ cups	bean sprouts, weighing about 4 oz
1	small bunch of Asian or regular basil
1	small cucumber

ORDER OF WORK

1 PREPARE THE CHICKEN

2 MAKE THE SALAD

3 PREPARE THE STIR-FRY VEGETABLES

4 STIR-FRY THE INGREDIENTS

1 PREPARE THE CHICKEN

1 With your fingers, pull off the skin from each of the chicken thighs. Remove and discard any fat and sinews.

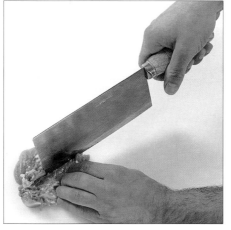

2 Using the cleaver, make a deep slit on the underside of each chicken thigh, along the length of the bone.

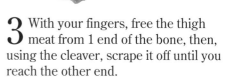

Grasp cleaver blade firmly

3 With your fingers, free the thigh meat from 1 end of the bone, then, using the cleaver, scrape it off until you reach the other end.

4 Cut the meat free from the bone. Trim any remaining fat and cut out the sinews from the meat.

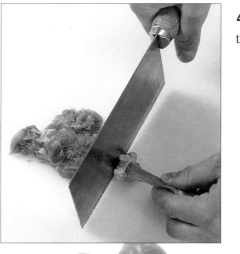

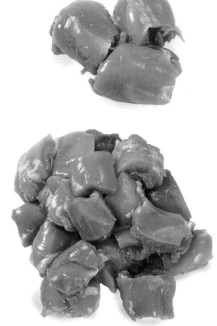

Cut good-sized pieces because they shrink during cooking

5 With the cleaver, cut the chicken meat into 1-inch strips, then cut across into 1-inch pieces.

6 Set the flat side of the cleaver on top of 1 garlic clove and strike it with your fist. Repeat with the remaining clove.

7 Discard the skin and finely chop the garlic. Peel and chop the lemon grass (see box, page 60).

8 For the marinade, combine the lemon grass, garlic, 2 tbsp fish sauce, and the black pepper in a large bowl and stir with the chopsticks until well mixed.

9 Add the pieces of chicken and toss until well coated with the marinade. Cover the bowl tightly and set aside to marinate, at least 1 hour or up to 24 hours.

ANNE SAYS
"If marinating the chicken for more than 1 hour, keep it in the refrigerator."

HOW TO PEEL AND CHOP LEMON GRASS

Lemon grass imparts a lovely lemony perfume to many Asian dishes. Because it is quite tough, it must be finely chopped.

1 Cut off and discard the dry leafy tops from the stalk of lemon grass, leaving about 6 inches of stalk.

2 Peel away any dry outer layers from the stalk until you reach the moist and tender core.

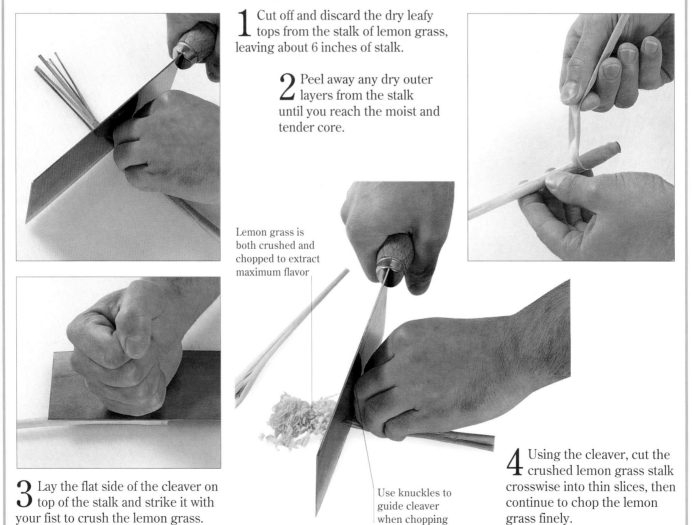

Lemon grass is both crushed and chopped to extract maximum flavor

Use knuckles to guide cleaver when chopping

3 Lay the flat side of the cleaver on top of the stalk and strike it with your fist to crush the lemon grass.

4 Using the cleaver, cut the crushed lemon grass stalk crosswise into thin slices, then continue to chop the lemon grass finely.

2 MAKE THE SALAD

1 Cut the core from the lettuce and separate the leaves. Wash the leaves in plenty of cold water; discard the tough stems. Dry the leaves in the salad spinner or on a dish towel.

Tear off tough lettuce stems with your fingers

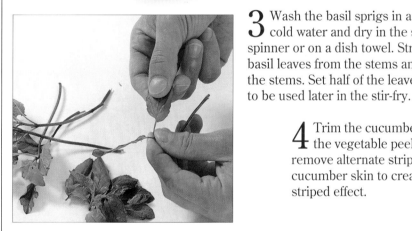

2 Pick over the bean sprouts, discarding any sprouts that are discolored. Remove the fine roots and any green hulls. Rinse the sprouts in cold running water in the colander and drain well.

3 Wash the basil sprigs in a bowl of cold water and dry in the salad spinner or on a dish towel. Strip the basil leaves from the stems and discard the stems. Set half of the leaves aside to be used later in the stir-fry.

4 Trim the cucumber. Using the vegetable peeler, remove alternate strips of the cucumber skin to create a striped effect.

6 Arrange the lettuce, bean sprouts, half of the basil leaves, and the cucumber in separate piles on a large platter. Cover tightly and chill.

Blade of cleaver makes it easy to transfer ingredients to platter

5 Cut the cucumber lengthwise in half. Set each cucumber half, cut-side down, on the chopping board, and cut across into thin slices.

Salad ingredients will remain crisp when chilled

3 PREPARE THE STIR-FRY VEGETABLES

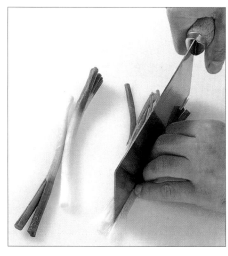

1 Trim the scallions, leaving some of the green tops. Slice each scallion lengthwise into thin strips.

Thinly cut scallion will soften quickly when stir-fried

2 Gather the scallion strips together with your fingers, and cut across into 1½-inch lengths.

3 Wearing rubber gloves, cut the chili peppers lengthwise in half, and discard the cores. Scrape out the seeds and cut away the fleshy white ribs from each half. Cut each half lengthwise into very thin strips.

4 Gather the strips together and cut them across into 1½-inch lengths.

4 STIR-FRY THE INGREDIENTS

1 Heat the wok over high heat until hot. Drizzle in the oil to coat the bottom and sides of the wok. Continue heating until the oil is hot.

Chicken will brown well if stir-fried over high heat

Hold wok steady with one hand while stir-frying

2 Add the chicken and marinade; stir-fry, stirring and tossing the mixture frequently, until the chicken is no longer pink, 8–10 minutes.

ANNE SAYS
"Boneless chicken breasts may be used instead of thighs. They will take only 4–5 minutes to cook."

3 Add the remaining fish sauce, the chili peppers, sugar, and scallions. Stir-fry, about 1 minute.

¶◎¶ TO SERVE
Serve the chicken with the salad. Each diner makes a bed of salad, tops it with chicken, and a few peanuts.

4 Add the remaining basil leaves, and toss quickly to mix with the chicken. Taste for seasoning, adding more fish sauce, if necessary.

Roasted peanuts add crunch to stir-fried chicken, which is spicy with chili peppers

VARIATION

LEMON GRASS PORK
MOO PAHT TAK RAI

Boneless pork loin is easy to cut for stir-frying. Serve this spicy dish with plain boiled long-grain rice as a more substantial alternative to the salad in the main recipe.

1 Omit the chicken, lettuce, bean sprouts, basil, and cucumber. Trim any fat and sinew from 1½ lb boneless pork loin and cut the pork across the grain into ¼-inch slices. Cut each slice into ¼-inch strips.

2 Prepare the marinade as directed and marinate the pork as for the chicken.
3 Stir-fry the pork as directed. Serve on a bed of boiled rice, decorated with sprigs of fresh coriander, if you like.

— **GETTING AHEAD** —
The chicken can be marinated up to 24 hours. The salad can be kept, covered, in the refrigerator. Stir-fry the chicken before serving.

CHINESE ROAST DUCK

Shao Ya

🍴 SERVES 4 🥢 WORK TIME 45 MINUTES* 🍲 ROASTING TIME 1¾–2 HOURS

EQUIPMENT

rack

wok †

cleaver ‡

bowls

roasting pan

paper towels

chopsticks

strainer

chopping board

pastry brush

wok scoop

6-inch bamboo skewer

kitchen string

† large deep saucepan can also be used

‡ chef's knife can also be used

INGREDIENTS

duck

light soy sauce

oil

fresh ginger root

maltose †

Szechwan peppercorns

ground bean sauce

Chinese rice wine ‡

five-spice powder

scallions

coriander

sugar

garlic cloves

† honey can also be used
‡ dry sherry can also be used

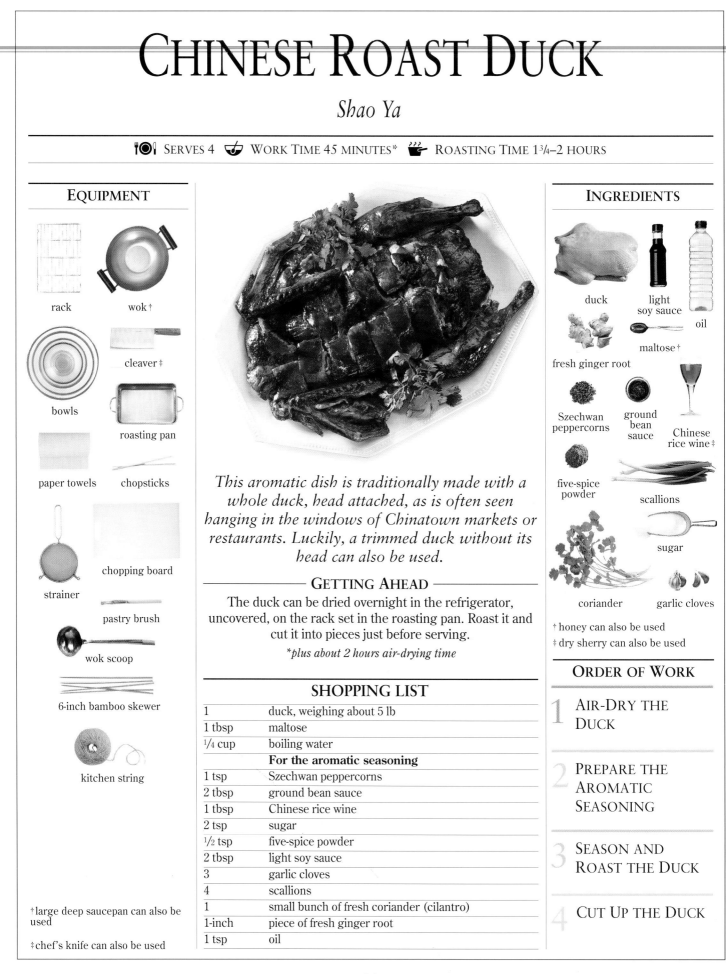

This aromatic dish is traditionally made with a whole duck, head attached, as is often seen hanging in the windows of Chinatown markets or restaurants. Luckily, a trimmed duck without its head can also be used.

GETTING AHEAD
The duck can be dried overnight in the refrigerator, uncovered, on the rack set in the roasting pan. Roast it and cut it into pieces just before serving.

*plus about 2 hours air-drying time

SHOPPING LIST

1	duck, weighing about 5 lb
1 tbsp	maltose
¼ cup	boiling water
For the aromatic seasoning	
1 tsp	Szechwan peppercorns
2 tbsp	ground bean sauce
1 tbsp	Chinese rice wine
2 tsp	sugar
½ tsp	five-spice powder
2 tbsp	light soy sauce
3	garlic cloves
4	scallions
1	small bunch of fresh coriander (cilantro)
1-inch	piece of fresh ginger root
1 tsp	oil

ORDER OF WORK

1 AIR-DRY THE DUCK

2 PREPARE THE AROMATIC SEASONING

3 SEASON AND ROAST THE DUCK

4 CUT UP THE DUCK

1 AIR-DRY THE DUCK

1 Rinse the duck thoroughly inside and out with cold water and pat dry with paper towels.

2 Pull away any visible fat from the body cavity and discard it. Tie heavy string around the flap of skin at the neck opening, looping it several times. If the neck has been trimmed too short to tie firmly, loop the string around both wings.

Leave an extra length of string to suspend duck

3 Half-fill the wok with water and bring to a boil. Hold the duck by the string and immerse it in the water. Using the wok scoop, pour water over the breast until the duck skin becomes taut, about 1 minute. Remove the duck and pat dry with paper towels.

! TAKE CARE !
If using a round-bottomed wok, place it on a wok ring for stability when boiling.

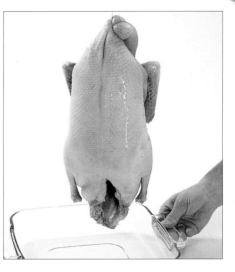

4 Hang the duck by the string in a cool (50–55°F), airy place. Place a dish underneath the duck to catch any drips. Leave until the skin is dry, about 2 hours. Meanwhile, prepare the aromatic seasoning.

ANNE SAYS
"An electric fan can be used to help dry the skin. Drying time with either method will vary depending on the weather."

2 PREPARE THE AROMATIC SEASONING

1 Heat the wok over medium heat until hot. Add the Szechwan peppercorns and cook, stirring with the chopsticks, until they smoke slightly, 1–2 minutes.

2 Transfer the peppercorns to a small sturdy bowl. With the handle of the cleaver, pound the peppercorns to a coarse powder.

4 Trim the scallions. Cut them across into 1-inch pieces, including the green tops. Strip the leaves from about half of the coriander stems. Pile the leaves on the chopping board and coarsely chop them using the cleaver. Reserve the remaining coriander sprigs for decoration.

Both white and green parts of scallions are used in Chinese cooking

3 Put the peppercorn powder in a medium bowl and add the bean sauce, rice wine, sugar, five-spice powder, and soy sauce. Stir together with the chopsticks to mix well.

Weight of cleaver makes chopping easy

5 Set the flat side of the cleaver on each garlic clove and strike it with your fist. Discard the skin and finely chop the garlic.

6 Scrape the skin from the ginger root, then slice it, cutting across the fibrous grain. Crush each of the slices with the flat of the cleaver, then finely chop the slices.

7 Heat the wok over medium heat until very hot. Drizzle in the oil to coat the bottom and sides. Continue heating until the oil is very hot, then add the garlic, ginger, and scallions, and stir-fry with the chopsticks until fragrant, about 30 seconds.

8 Add the bean sauce mixture and chopped coriander to the wok. Bring to a boil, then reduce the heat to low, and simmer, about 1 minute. Transfer the seasoning to a bowl and let cool to room temperature.

Simmering allows flavors to blend

3 SEASON AND ROAST THE DUCK

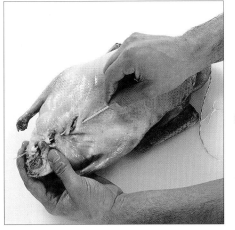

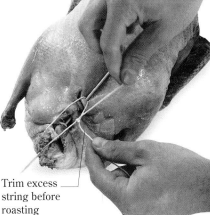

Trim excess string before roasting

1 About 45 minutes before roasting the duck, put the bamboo skewer into a bowl of cold water, and let soak. Heat the oven to 400°F. Spoon the aromatic seasoning into the body cavity of the duck.

2 Overlap the skin to close the cavity and thread the skewer 2–3 times from the top of the cavity through both layers of skin, then through the tail.

3 To close tightly, tie the string around the tail and the top of the skewer to bring the tail up. Set the duck, breast-side up, on the rack set in the roasting pan. Roast the duck in the heated oven, 15 minutes.

Duck develops rich mahogany color during roasting

Once duck is cooked, leg meat gives easily when pinched

4 Meanwhile, combine the maltose and boiling water in a small bowl, stirring with the chopsticks to dissolve the maltose completely. Remove the duck from the oven, and brush the maltose mixture generously all over the skin of the duck.

5 Reduce the oven temperature to 350°F and continue roasting, brushing every 15 minutes with the maltose mixture, until the duck is dark brown and the leg meat feels soft when pinched, 1½–1¾ hours.

6 Transfer the roasted duck to the chopping board and let stand, about 15 minutes, then carefully remove the string and skewer.

7 Set the strainer over a bowl. Pour the seasoning from the duck cavity into the strainer. Skim off and discard the fat from the seasoning liquid; reserve the liquid.

4 CUT UP THE DUCK

1 Place the duck, breast-side up, on the chopping board. With the cleaver, cut the wings from the body, separating them at the shoulder joints.

Pull wing bone away from body of duck to help locate joint

ANNE SAYS
"For greater control when cutting through bone with the cleaver, hold the blade against the bone and strike it with a hammer or mallet. Alternatively, use poultry shears to cut up the duck."

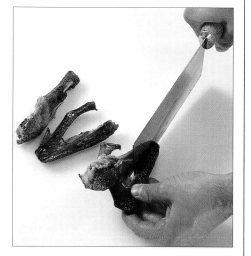

2 Cut each wing in half across the middle joint, leaving the wing tip attached if present.

3 Cut off the legs through the thigh joints, close to the body.

4 Cut through both of the leg joints to separate the drumsticks from the thigh portions.

5 Cut the thighs crosswise, through the bone, into 1-inch pieces.

6 Arrange the wings, thigh slices, and drumsticks around the rim of a warmed serving platter to resemble the shape of the duck.

Choose a platter large enough to hold whole carved duck

7 Cut the duck through the rib bones to split the body carcass lengthwise in half so the back and breast are cut into 2 separate pieces.

! TAKE CARE !
Hold the duck carcass firmly so it does not slip while being cut in half.

8 Cut the back of the duck across into 1-inch pieces. Slide the cleaver blade underneath the slices to transfer them to the platter. Arrange the back pieces lengthwise down the center of the platter.

Flat blade of cleaver transfers sliced breast meat neatly to platter

9 Cut through the breastbone lengthwise to split the breast, then cut each half across into 1-inch slices. Slide the cleaver underneath the breast slices to lift, and place them over the back slices on the platter.

🍴 TO SERVE
Pour the seasoning drained from the cavity over the duck, if you like, and decorate the platter with the reserved coriander sprigs. Serve immediately.

Traditional Chinese roast duck is deeply colored, crisp, and fragrant with spice

Duck is cut into small pieces, for easy handling with chopsticks

CANTONESE ROAST CHICKEN

SHAO JI

In China, roast chicken is often purchased from markets since kitchens frequently lack ovens.

1 Omit the duck, Szechwan peppercorns, scallions, fresh coriander, and maltose basting mixture. Prepare a 4-lb chicken, but do not pour boiling water over the bird or air-dry it.
2 Finely chop the garlic and stir-fry, 5 seconds. Add 1/2 cup hoisin sauce, 1/3 cup water, and 1 tsp dark sesame oil with the bean sauce, rice wine, sugar, five-spice powder, and soy sauce. Bring to a boil, simmer, and cool as directed.
3 Heat the oven to 350°F. Spoon 3 tbsp of the seasoning into the chicken cavity and skewer it as directed. Set the chicken on a rack in a roasting pan. Brush with 3 tbsp of the seasoning, add 1 1/2 cups water to the pan.
4 Roast, 45 minutes, add 1 1/2 cups more water, then cover loosely with foil. Continue roasting, brushing 2–3 times with seasoning, until the juices from the thighs run clear, about 1 1/4 hours longer. If all the water evaporates during cooking, add 1 cup more to keep the juices from burning.
5 Remove the skewer; pour the cavity juices into a saucepan. Let the chicken stand, then cut up as directed.
6 Pour the drippings from the roasting pan into the juices in the saucepan and skim off the fat. Stir in the remaining seasoning and bring to a boil.
7 Serve the chicken on a bed of boiled rice, decorated with coriander sprigs; pass the sauce separately.

YELLOW FLOWER PORK

Mu Shu Rou

🍽 SERVES 4 🥣 WORK TIME 35–45 MINUTES* 🍲 COOKING TIME 15–20 MINUTES

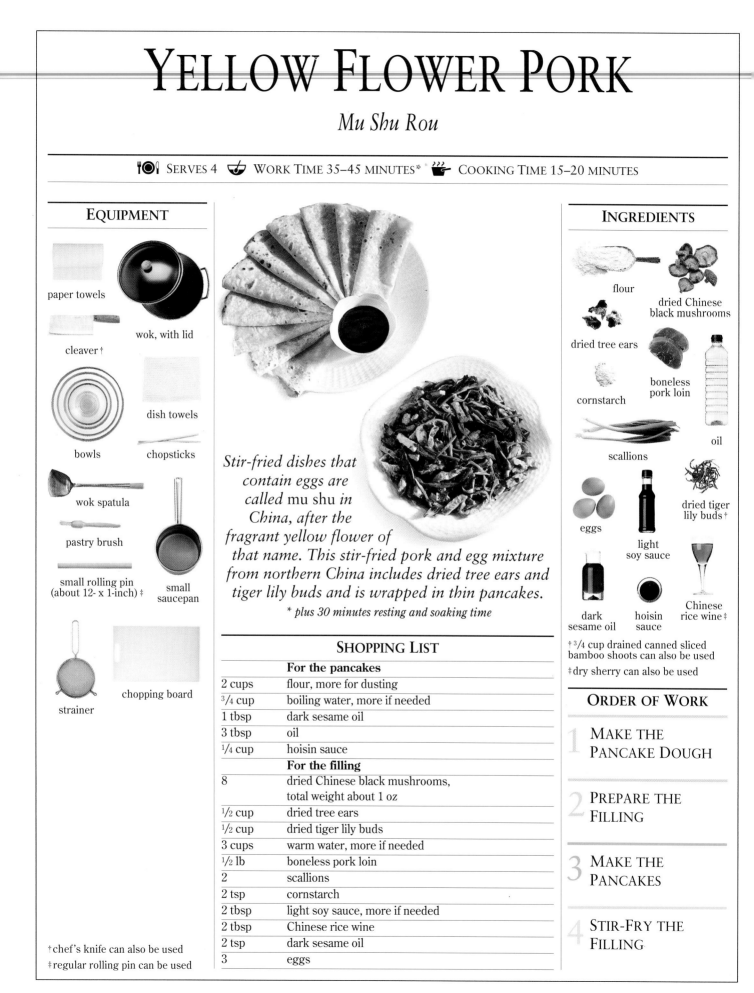

EQUIPMENT

paper towels

cleaver †

wok, with lid

bowls

dish towels

chopsticks

wok spatula

pastry brush

small rolling pin
(about 12- x 1-inch) ‡

small
saucepan

strainer

chopping board

† chef's knife can also be used

‡ regular rolling pin can be used

INGREDIENTS

flour

dried Chinese
black mushrooms

dried tree ears

cornstarch

boneless
pork loin

oil

scallions

eggs

light
soy sauce

dried tiger
lily buds †

dark
sesame oil

hoisin
sauce

Chinese
rice wine ‡

† ³/₄ cup drained canned sliced
bamboo shoots can also be used

‡ dry sherry can also be used

Stir-fried dishes that contain eggs are called mu shu *in China, after the fragrant yellow flower of that name. This stir-fried pork and egg mixture from northern China includes dried tree ears and tiger lily buds and is wrapped in thin pancakes.*

* plus 30 minutes resting and soaking time

SHOPPING LIST

	For the pancakes
2 cups	flour, more for dusting
³/₄ cup	boiling water, more if needed
1 tbsp	dark sesame oil
3 tbsp	oil
¹/₄ cup	hoisin sauce
	For the filling
8	dried Chinese black mushrooms, total weight about 1 oz
¹/₂ cup	dried tree ears
¹/₂ cup	dried tiger lily buds
3 cups	warm water, more if needed
¹/₂ lb	boneless pork loin
2	scallions
2 tsp	cornstarch
2 tbsp	light soy sauce, more if needed
2 tbsp	Chinese rice wine
2 tsp	dark sesame oil
3	eggs

ORDER OF WORK

1 **MAKE THE PANCAKE DOUGH**

2 **PREPARE THE FILLING**

3 **MAKE THE PANCAKES**

4 **STIR-FRY THE FILLING**

1 MAKE THE PANCAKE DOUGH

Dough is pliable and kneads easily

1 Put the flour into a large bowl and make a well in the center. Slowly pour the boiling water into the well, mixing in the flour with the chopsticks. Continue mixing until the water is absorbed and the mixture forms a rough mass.

2 Let stand until cool enough to handle, about 1 minute. Gather the dough together and press into a ball.

ANNE SAYS
"If necessary, add 1 tbsp more boiling water so the dough holds together."

3 Turn the dough onto a lightly floured surface and knead it, adding more flour as necessary, until it is smooth and elastic, about 5 minutes. Cover loosely with a dish towel, and let rest, 30 minutes. Meanwhile, prepare the filling ingredients.

2 PREPARE THE FILLING

1 Put the black mushrooms, tree ears, and tiger lily buds in separate bowls. Cover each with 1 cup warm water, and let soak, 30 minutes.

3 Trim the scallions, leaving some green tops. Cut the scallions lengthwise into thin strips. Stack the strips and cut them crosswise into 2-inch lengths.

Thinly cut strips will cook quickly in stir-fry

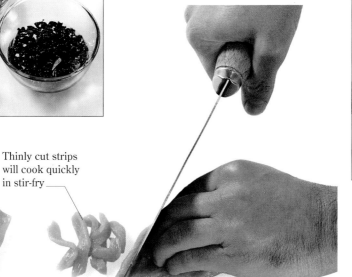

Thin strips of pork will cook quickly and be tender

2 Trim off any fat from the pork. With the cleaver, cut it crosswise into ¼-inch slices. Cut each slice into ⅛-inch strips.

4 Drain the black mushrooms, reserving the liquid. Trim off the hard, woody stems, then slice the mushroom caps.

5 Line the strainer with paper towels and hold it over a measuring cup. Pour in the mushroom soaking liquid to strain; reserve ½ cup of the mushroom liquid.

6 Put the cornstarch into a small bowl. Add the reserved mushroom liquid, and mix together with the chopsticks until smooth. Then stir in the soy sauce, rice wine, and sesame oil.

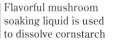

Flavorful mushroom soaking liquid is used to dissolve cornstarch

Rice wine is classic seasoning for pork mixture

7 Drain the tree ears and tiger lily buds separately in the strainer and rinse well with water to remove any grit. Drain, and squeeze them dry. Cut off and discard the tough ends.

Eggs are easy to mix with chopsticks

8 Chop the softened tree ears into small pieces if necessary.

9 In a small bowl, beat the eggs together with the chopsticks until well mixed.

3 MAKE THE PANCAKES

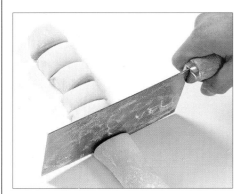

1 On a lightly floured surface, roll out the dough into a cylinder about 12 inches long. Dust the cleaver with flour, and cut the cylinder across into 12 equal pieces. Cover the pieces with a lightly dampened dish towel.

2 Dust your palms with flour, and roll each piece of dough into a ball in the palms of your hands. Flatten each ball to make a 3-inch round, and cover again with the dampened dish towel.

3 Put the sesame oil in a small bowl. Brush 1 side of each round lightly with oil. Press the oiled sides of 2 rounds together to form 6 pairs of rounds. Lightly flour the work surface and rolling pin. Roll out each pair of dough rounds into a thin pancake, about 7 inches in diameter, turning the pancake over frequently and rolling evenly on both sides.

Rounds are rolled to cook in pairs so they stay moist

Be sure pancake is evenly rolled out flat

! TAKE CARE !

Do not roll the edges too thin or the 2 halves of the pancake will be difficult to separate after cooking and may tear.

Wok spatula has curved edge so is ideal for turning pancakes

4 Heat the wok until very hot. Add 1 pancake and cook until slightly blistered and puffed, about 1 minute. Turn with the wok spatula and cook the other side, pressing down with the spatula until brown spots appear on the underside, about 30 seconds longer.

5 Remove the pancake from the wok with the spatula, then peel the halves apart to make 2 very thin pancakes. Repeat with the remainder. Once the pancakes are cooked, stack them on a plate; cover with a dampened dish towel to keep warm.

4 STIR-FRY THE FILLING

1 Heat the wok over medium heat until hot. Drizzle in 1 tbsp oil to coat the bottom and sides of the wok. Continue heating until the oil is hot, then pour in the eggs. Tilt the wok so the eggs spread out in an even layer. Cook to form a thin omelet, set in the center and slightly crisp around the edge, about 2 minutes.

Rotate wok to swirl eggs evenly

2 With the wok spatula, carefully turn the omelet over. Cook until the other side is lightly browned, 15–30 seconds longer.

3 Slide the omelet onto the chopping board with the wok spatula. Let cool slightly. Roll it up loosely, and with the cleaver, cut it crosswise into ¼-inch strips.

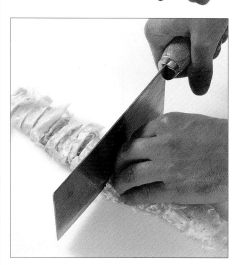

4 Reheat the wok over high heat. Drizzle in the remaining oil and continue heating until very hot. Add the pork and cook, stirring and tossing, until the pork is no longer pink, 2–3 minutes.

5 Add the tree ears, tiger lily buds, and Chinese black mushrooms to the wok, and stir-fry with the pork until mixed and heated through.

Tiger lily buds and tree ears are added to stir-fry for their chewy texture

6 With the chopsticks, stir the cornstarch mixture again, then pour it into the pork mixture.

7 Stir-fry, using the wok spatula, until the vegetables are very hot and the cornstarch thickens the sauce slightly, about 2 minutes.

8 Add the scallions and omelet strips and taste for seasoning, adding more soy sauce if needed. Stir-fry until very hot, about 1 minute longer.

🍴◉ TO SERVE

Spoon the filling into a warmed serving dish. Fold the warm pancakes in half and arrange on a plate. Put the hoisin sauce in a small bowl. Each diner spreads a little sauce onto a pancake, tops it with some filling, and rolls it up.

Scallions add zest to the earthy flavor of the pork, egg, and mushroom stir-fry

Sesame-flavored pancakes are brushed with hoisin sauce to wrap pork mixture

GETTING AHEAD

The pancakes can be made 1 day ahead and kept, layered with wax paper and tightly wrapped, in the refrigerator. To reheat, arrange them overlapping in a bamboo steamer basket and steam 2–3 minutes over boiling water. The filling ingredients can be prepared up to 1 hour ahead; stir-fry them together just before serving.

VARIATION

YELLOW FLOWER VEGETABLES

MU SHU TS'AI

Nutritious tofu replaces the pork in this vegetarian version of Mu Shu Rou.

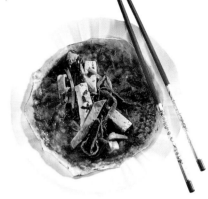

1 Make the pancakes as directed in the main recipe.

2 Omit the pork. Prepare the filling ingredients and the omelet as directed.

3 Rinse and drain 1/2 lb firm tofu; pat dry with paper towels. Lay the tofu on a chopping board and cut it across into 1/2-inch slices. Stack the slices, and cut into 1/2-inch strips. Lightly dust the strips with 2–3 tbsp cornstarch.

4 Reheat the wok over medium-high heat until very hot. Drizzle in 2 tbsp oil to coat the bottom and sides; continue heating until the oil is very hot. Add the tofu strips. Fry, without stirring, until lightly browned on one side, about 5 minutes. Carefully turn over the tofu and brown the other side. Transfer the tofu from the wok to a plate and set aside.

5 Reheat the wok, add the tree ears, tiger lily buds, and black mushrooms, and stir-fry, about 2 minutes. Add the cornstarch mixture; cook, stirring, until the sauce thickens, 2–3 minutes.

6 Add the scallions, omelet strips, and tofu, and toss gently. Taste for seasoning, adding more soy sauce if needed, and serve as directed.

INDONESIAN CURRIED BEEF

Rendang Daging

🍽 SERVES 6 ⏲ WORK TIME 40–50 MINUTES 🍲 COOKING TIME 3½–4 HOURS

EQUIPMENT

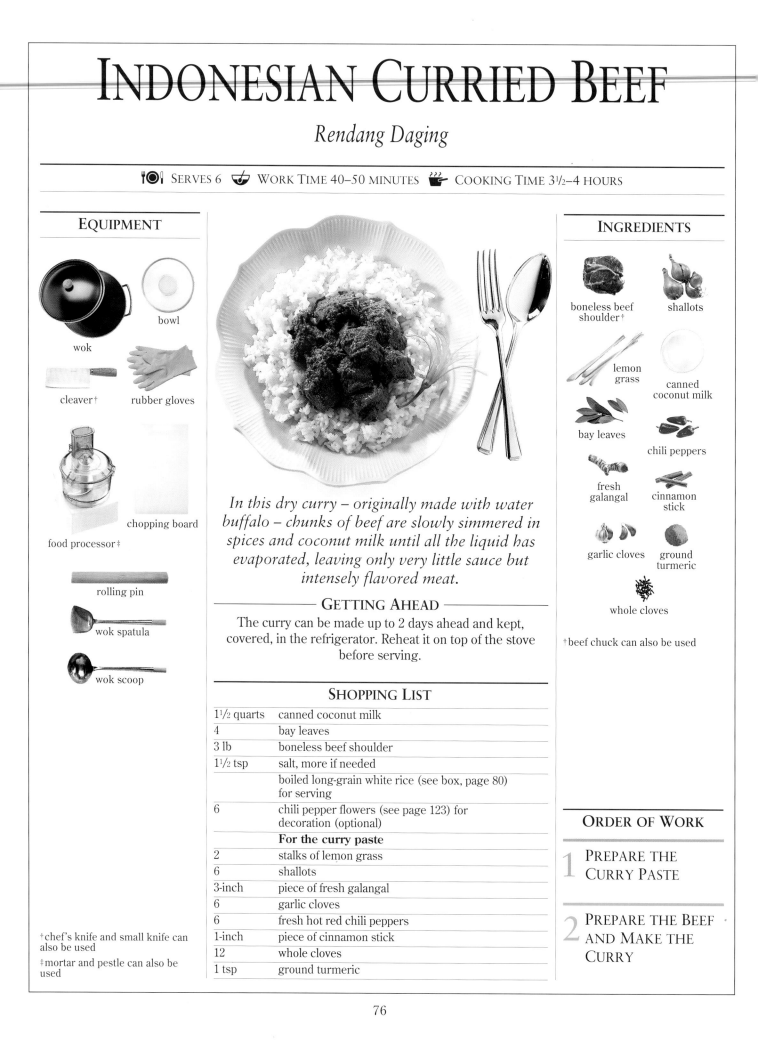

wok

bowl

cleaver†

rubber gloves

food processor‡

chopping board

rolling pin

wok spatula

wok scoop

INGREDIENTS

boneless beef shoulder†

shallots

lemon grass

canned coconut milk

bay leaves

chili peppers

fresh galangal

cinnamon stick

garlic cloves

ground turmeric

whole cloves

†beef chuck can also be used

In this dry curry – originally made with water buffalo – chunks of beef are slowly simmered in spices and coconut milk until all the liquid has evaporated, leaving only very little sauce but intensely flavored meat.

GETTING AHEAD

The curry can be made up to 2 days ahead and kept, covered, in the refrigerator. Reheat it on top of the stove before serving.

SHOPPING LIST

1½ quarts	canned coconut milk
4	bay leaves
3 lb	boneless beef shoulder
1½ tsp	salt, more if needed
	boiled long-grain white rice (see box, page 80) for serving
6	chili pepper flowers (see page 123) for decoration (optional)
	For the curry paste
2	stalks of lemon grass
6	shallots
3-inch	piece of fresh galangal
6	garlic cloves
6	fresh hot red chili peppers
1-inch	piece of cinnamon stick
12	whole cloves
1 tsp	ground turmeric

ORDER OF WORK

1 PREPARE THE CURRY PASTE

2 PREPARE THE BEEF AND MAKE THE CURRY

†chef's knife and small knife can also be used

‡mortar and pestle can also be used

1 PREPARE THE CURRY PASTE

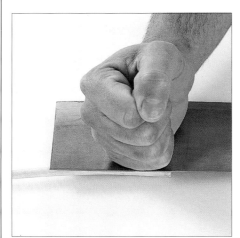

Shallots are later finely chopped in food processor

1 Cut off the dry leafy tops from the stalks of lemon grass. Peel away any dry outer layers until you reach the moist and tender core. Crush the lemon grass stalks with the flat side of the cleaver, then cut the stalks crosswise into 1-inch pieces.

2 Peel the shallots and separate into sections if necessary. Trim the root ends and cut the shallots into quarters.

3 With the cleaver, trim any stems or knobs from the galangal and scrape off the skin. Slice the galangal, cutting across the fibrous grain.

4 Place the flat side of the cleaver on each slice of galangal and strike it with your fist, then roughly chop.

5 Set the flat side of the cleaver on top of each garlic clove and strike it with your fist. Discard the skin. Finely dice the chili peppers (see box, page 78).

6 Crumble or break the cinnamon stick into small pieces and put them in the small bowl with the cloves. Pound them with the end of the rolling pin or the cleaver handle until they are coarsely crushed.

Spices make assertive, fresh curry paste

7 Put the cinnamon and cloves in the food processor with the lemon grass, shallots, galangal, chili peppers, turmeric, and garlic. Process the ingredients to make a coarse paste. If the mixture is very thick, add 3–4 tablespoons of the coconut milk.

ANNE SAYS
"Alternatively, you can make the curry paste in a mortar and pestle. First finely chop all the ingredients. Put each one in the mortar and pound it to a coarse paste before adding the next ingredient."

2 PREPARE THE BEEF AND MAKE THE CURRY

1 Combine the curry paste and coconut milk in the wok and stir until well mixed. Add the bay leaves and bring to a boil over high heat, stirring occasionally.

2 Reduce the heat to medium and cook the sauce, stirring occasionally with the wok spatula, about 15 minutes.

Be sure to wear rubber gloves and to avoid contact with eyes because hot chili peppers can burn your hands and eyes.

1 Cut the chili pepper lengthwise in half. Cut out the core and white ribs; scrape out the seeds.

2 Set each half of chili pepper cut-side up and thinly slice it lengthwise.

3 Gather the strips together in a pile with your fingers and cut across into very fine dice.

3 Meanwhile, with the cleaver, trim off the fat and sinew from the beef and cut it into 1½- to 2-inch cubes.

4 Add the beef and salt to the curry sauce, stir, and return to a boil over high heat. Reduce the heat to medium and simmer, uncovered, stirring occasionally, 2 hours.

5 Reduce the heat to very low and continue cooking until the beef is tender and the sauce is quite thick, 1½–2 hours. Stir frequently to prevent the curry from sticking to the wok.

6 Skim off all the fat from the curried beef, using the wok scoop. Taste the curry and add salt if necessary.

ANNE SAYS
"The curry will be very thick and rich. Toward the end of cooking, oil will separate from the sauce and the beef will fry in it."

¡☺¡ TO SERVE
Arrange a bed of rice on warmed individual plates or in shallow bowls, and spoon the curried beef on top. Decorate each serving with a chili pepper flower, if you like.

Dry beef curry is made by long slow cooking so most of the liquid evaporates

Fluffed white rice is traditional accompaniment to curries

BOILED LONG-GRAIN WHITE RICE

Rice is a staple in all Asian cuisines because it is highly nutritious and a suitable foil for intensely flavored dishes. Perfect rice – with separate grains – is achievable every time using this method.

🍴 SERVES 6

🥄 WORK TIME 5 MINUTES

🍲 COOKING TIME 15–20 MINUTES*

* plus 15 minutes standing time

SHOPPING LIST

2 cups	long-grain white rice
3 cups	water

1 Put the rice in a bowl, cover with cold water, and stir with your fingertips until the water turns milky-white. Pour off the water.

2 Repeat the process once or twice until the water is fairly clear. Drain the rice in a strainer.

Strain starchy water from rice

3 Put the rice in a saucepan and add the measured water. Bring to a boil over high heat. Stir the rice with chopsticks. Cover the pan, and reduce the heat to low. Simmer until all the water has been absorbed and the rice is tender, about 15 minutes.

4 Take from the heat and let the rice stand, without lifting the lid, about 15 minutes. Uncover and stir the rice with the chopsticks to fluff it.

Chopsticks fluff grains without making rice sticky

Rice grains are fully cooked and separate

VARIATION

VIETNAMESE STEWED BEEF

THIT BO KNO

In Vietnam, this beef stew is eaten with French bread, a carryover from the country's colonial past.

Juicy carrots add golden color to beef stew

1 Omit the galangal, cinnamon stick, whole cloves, turmeric, and coconut milk. Prepare a 1-inch piece of fresh ginger root as directed for galangal. Prepare the lemon grass, shallots, garlic, and 2 fresh hot red chili peppers as directed.

2 Cut the beef into cubes as directed. In a large bowl, combine the ginger, lemon grass, shallots, garlic, and chili peppers. Stir in 3 tbsp fish sauce, 2 tsp ground cinnamon, 2 tsp curry powder, and 2 tsp sugar.

5 Heat the wok over high heat until very hot. Drizzle in 1 tbsp oil to coat the bottom and sides of the wok. Continue heating until the oil is very hot, then add one-third of the marinated beef and stir-fry until well browned on all sides, 5–7 minutes. Transfer the beef to a bowl.

6 Reheat the wok, add more oil, and brown the remaining beef and marinade in 2 more batches. Transfer the beef and juices to the bowl.

7 Reheat the wok, then add the onion slices and stir-fry, 1 minute. Return all the browned beef and its juices to the wok. Add 3 whole star anise, ¼ cup tomato paste, 1 quart water, and stir well to mix. Bring to a boil, cover, and simmer over low heat, about 1½ hours, stirring occasionally.

8 Add the carrots and continue cooking until

beef and carrots are tender, 45–60 minutes longer. The stew should be rich, but not too thick. Remove and discard the star anise. Serve the stew hot, decorated with fresh basil leaves, and accompanied by French bread.

3 Add the beef cubes and mix well with your hands, then let marinate, about 30 minutes.

4 Meanwhile, peel 1 large onion, leaving a little of the root attached, and cut it in half through the root and stem. Lay each half flat on a chopping board and cut across into thin slices. Peel 6 carrots and cut them lengthwise in half, then cut the halves crosswise into 2-inch pieces.

Star anise adds exotic spice flavor to beef

KOREAN GRILLED BEEF

Bulgogi

🍴 SERVES 4 🥣 WORK TIME 50 MINUTES* 🍲 COOKING TIME 10 MINUTES

EQUIPMENT

table-top brazier

cleaver †

chopsticks

pastry brush

colander

bowls

electric spice grinder ‡

pepper mill

vegetable peeler

small frying pan

jar, with airtight lid

chopping board

†chef's knife can also be used

‡mortar and pestle can also be used

ANNE SAYS

"A Korean bulgogi is a dome-shaped metal hotplate that sits directly over a table-top burner. A broiler pan and rack can be used as a substitute."

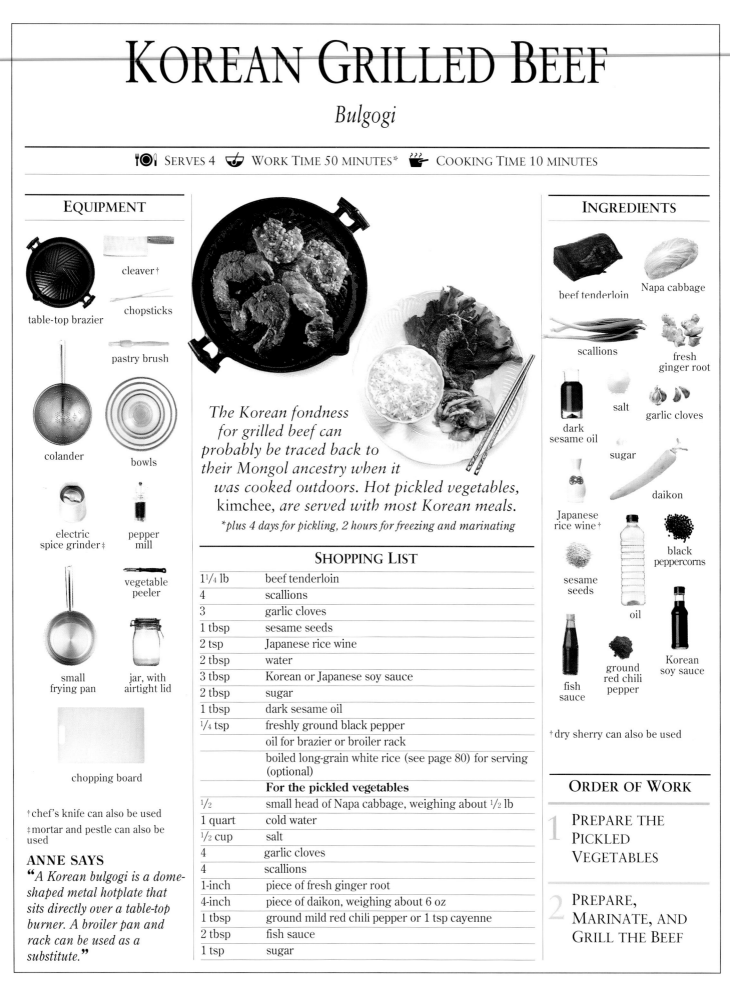

The Korean fondness for grilled beef can probably be traced back to their Mongol ancestry when it was cooked outdoors. Hot pickled vegetables, kimchee, are served with most Korean meals.

*plus 4 days for pickling, 2 hours for freezing and marinating

SHOPPING LIST

1¼ lb	beef tenderloin
4	scallions
3	garlic cloves
1 tbsp	sesame seeds
2 tsp	Japanese rice wine
2 tbsp	water
3 tbsp	Korean or Japanese soy sauce
2 tbsp	sugar
1 tbsp	dark sesame oil
¼ tsp	freshly ground black pepper
	oil for brazier or broiler rack
	boiled long-grain white rice (see page 80) for serving (optional)
For the pickled vegetables	
½	small head of Napa cabbage, weighing about ½ lb
1 quart	cold water
½ cup	salt
4	garlic cloves
4	scallions
1-inch	piece of fresh ginger root
4-inch	piece of daikon, weighing about 6 oz
1 tbsp	ground mild red chili pepper or 1 tsp cayenne
2 tbsp	fish sauce
1 tsp	sugar

INGREDIENTS

beef tenderloin

Napa cabbage

scallions

fresh ginger root

dark sesame oil

salt

garlic cloves

sugar

Japanese rice wine †

daikon

sesame seeds

oil

black peppercorns

fish sauce

ground red chili pepper

Korean soy sauce

† dry sherry can also be used

ORDER OF WORK

1 PREPARE THE PICKLED VEGETABLES

2 PREPARE, MARINATE, AND GRILL THE BEEF

1 PREPARE THE PICKLED VEGETABLES

1 Rinse the cabbage in cold water. Put the measured water and all but ¼ tsp of the salt in a large bowl and stir until the salt has dissolved. Add the cabbage and weight it with a plate to keep it covered. Let soak, 8–10 hours.

2 Set the flat side of the cleaver on each garlic clove and strike it with your fist. Discard the skin and finely chop the garlic. Trim the scallions, leaving some of the green tops. Cut across and coarsely chop.

Coarsely chopped scallions will release flavor

3 Scrape the skin from the ginger root with the cleaver. Slice the ginger, cutting across the fibrous grain. Crush each slice with the flat of the cleaver, then finely chop the slices.

4 Peel the daikon with the vegetable peeler, and cut it crosswise in half. Cut each half lengthwise into ⅛-inch slices. Stack the slices and cut into ⅛-inch strips.

5 In a bowl, mix the chili pepper or cayenne with the fish sauce, sugar, and the remaining salt, using the chopsticks. Add the garlic, scallions, ginger, and daikon strips and stir well until the mixture is red in color.

6 Drain the cabbage, rinse with cold water, and squeeze it between your hands to remove all the moisture. Place the wilted cabbage, cut-side up, on the work surface. Beginning with the large bottom leaves, pack the daikon mixture between each leaf.

Keep cabbage leaves attached at core while layering with daikon mixture

7 Fold the cabbage leaves and push them into the jar. Pour any leftover daikon mixture on top. Cover with the lid, and leave in a cool place to ferment, at least 3 days. The cabbage will wilt and produce liquid.

Push folded cabbage into jar with chopsticks

8 Each day, open the jar to release any gas. Push the cabbage down into the liquid in the jar. After 3 days, taste a cabbage leaf to test if it is sufficiently sour.

9 When ready, put the cabbage on the chopping board and cut it crosswise into 1-inch slices. Pile the vegetables into a bowl, cover, and refrigerate until ready to serve.

Cut cabbage into generous slices

2 PREPARE, MARINATE, AND GRILL THE BEEF

1 Wrap the piece of beef and freeze, about 1 hour. Meanwhile, prepare the marinade ingredients. Trim the scallions, leaving some of the green tops, then cut crosswise and coarsely chop them.

2 Set the flat side of the cleaver on top of each garlic clove and strike it with your fist. Discard the skin and finely chop the garlic.

3 Heat the frying pan over medium-high heat. Add the sesame seeds and cook, stirring constantly, until golden brown, 1–2 minutes. Transfer the toasted sesame seeds to the spice grinder and work until fine but not reduced to a paste. Alternatively, crush the seeds with a mortar and pestle.

Sesame seeds are fragrant when toasted

ANNE SAYS
"Crushing sesame seeds releases their full flavor."

4 Combine the scallions, garlic, toasted sesame seeds, rice wine, water, soy sauce, sugar, sesame oil, and pepper in a bowl and stir well with chopsticks to mix.

Thinly sliced beef
quickly absorbs
flavor of marinade

5 When the beef is partially frozen, cut it across the grain into ¼-inch slices. Arrange the beef slices, overlapping, on a large plate.

6 Pour the marinade over the beef slices. Cover the plate tightly and let marinate at room temperature, about 1 hour.

7 Lightly oil the cooking surface of the table-top brazier. Heat the brazier over high heat until sizzling and very hot.

ANNE SAYS
"If grilling the beef outdoors, prepare the grill ahead, so it is very hot when you are ready to cook."

8 Arrange as many slices of the marinated beef as will fit in a single layer on the brazier. Cook the beef until well-browned, about 1 minute. Turn over the slices and brown the other side, about 1 minute longer. They should remain pink in the center.

🍽 **TO SERVE**
Each diner takes a slice of beef directly from the brazier, to eat with the pickled vegetables and plain boiled rice. Continue cooking the remaining beef when the first batch is finished.

Tender beef cooks
in just a few minutes

Rice balances piquant flavor
of pickled cabbage

— **GETTING AHEAD** —
The pickled vegetables can be made up to 2 weeks ahead, and kept in the refrigerator. The beef slices and marinade can be prepared up to 3 hours ahead and kept separately, covered, in the refrigerator. Marinate the beef 1 hour before serving.

MALAYSIAN FRIED RICE NOODLES

Char Kway Teow

🍽️ SERVES 4 🥄 WORK TIME 30 – 40 MINUTES 🍲 COOKING TIME 8–12 MINUTES

EQUIPMENT

colander

wok

wok spatula

rubber gloves

bowls

cleaver†

paper towels

medium saucepan

chopping board

† chef's knife can also be used

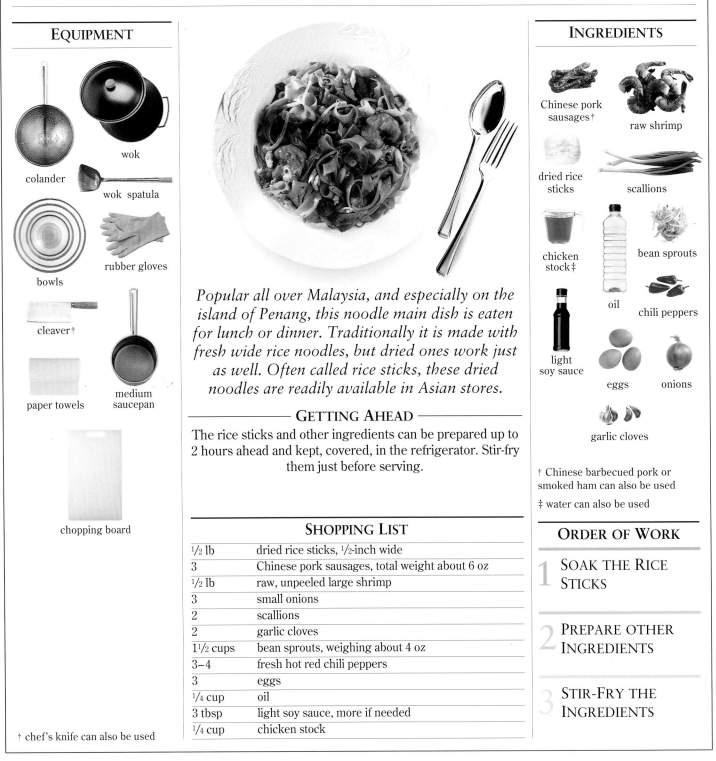

Popular all over Malaysia, and especially on the island of Penang, this noodle main dish is eaten for lunch or dinner. Traditionally it is made with fresh wide rice noodles, but dried ones work just as well. Often called rice sticks, these dried noodles are readily available in Asian stores.

GETTING AHEAD

The rice sticks and other ingredients can be prepared up to 2 hours ahead and kept, covered, in the refrigerator. Stir-fry them just before serving.

SHOPPING LIST

½ lb	dried rice sticks, ½-inch wide
3	Chinese pork sausages, total weight about 6 oz
½ lb	raw, unpeeled large shrimp
3	small onions
2	scallions
2	garlic cloves
1½ cups	bean sprouts, weighing about 4 oz
3–4	fresh hot red chili peppers
3	eggs
¼ cup	oil
3 tbsp	light soy sauce, more if needed
¼ cup	chicken stock

INGREDIENTS

Chinese pork sausages†

raw shrimp

dried rice sticks

scallions

chicken stock‡

bean sprouts

oil

chili peppers

light soy sauce

eggs

onions

garlic cloves

† Chinese barbecued pork or smoked ham can also be used

‡ water can also be used

ORDER OF WORK

1 SOAK THE RICE STICKS

2 PREPARE OTHER INGREDIENTS

3 STIR-FRY THE INGREDIENTS

1 SOAK THE RICE STICKS

1 Put the rice sticks in a bowl and cover with warm water. Let soak until soft, about 30 minutes. Meanwhile, prepare the other ingredients.

2 Thoroughly drain the softened rice sticks in the colander and set aside.

2 PREPARE OTHER INGREDIENTS

1 With the cleaver, cut the Chinese sausages diagonally into thin slices. Peel and devein the shrimp (see box, right).

ANNE SAYS
"*If the sausage has a thick skin, peel it off before slicing. If using Chinese barbecued pork or smoked ham, cut it into 1-inch strips.*"

Sausage slices will mix well with other ingredients

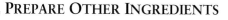

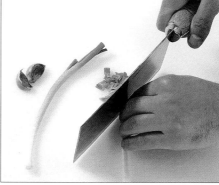

2 Peel the onions, leaving a little of the root attached. Cut a thin slice from one side so each onion sits firmly on the chopping board, and cut each onion across into thin rings. Separate the rings with your fingers.

3 Trim the scallions and cut them diagonally into ¼-inch slices, including some of their green tops.

HOW TO PEEL AND DEVEIN SHRIMP

A sharp cleaver is ideal for making a clean cut when deveining shrimp. For efficiency, peel all the shrimp at once, then cut them all, and finally remove all the veins.

1 Peel off the shell from the shrimp with your fingers. Discard the shell.

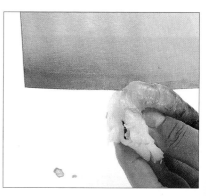

2 Roll the blade of a cleaver along the back of the shrimp to make a shallow cut.

3 Gently pull out the dark intestinal vein and discard it. Rinse the shrimp, and pat dry with paper towels.

4 Set the flat side of the cleaver on top of each garlic clove and strike it with your fist. Peel the skin from the garlic clove and discard it. Finely chop the garlic.

5 Pick over the bean sprouts, discarding any that are discolored. Rinse the sprouts in cold water and drain well.

6 Wearing rubber gloves, halve the chili peppers lengthwise; discard the cores. Scrape out the seeds and cut away the fleshy white ribs. Cut into very thin strips. Gather the strips and cut across to make fine dice.

3 STIR-FRY THE INGREDIENTS

2 Increase the heat to medium-high, and add the remaining oil. When the oil is hot, add the onions and stir-fry, tossing with the wok spatula, until they start to brown, 3–4 minutes. Add the chili peppers, garlic, and Chinese sausages and stir-fry until fragrant, about 30 seconds.

White rice sticks will color during stir-frying

1 Beat the eggs in a bowl. Heat the wok over medium heat until hot. Drizzle in 1 tbsp of the oil to coat the bottom and sides. Continue heating until the oil is hot, pour in the beaten eggs, and stir at once with the wok spatula, until the eggs are scrambled in small pieces, 1–2 minutes. Transfer the eggs to a bowl and set aside.

Tender shrimp cooks quickly

4 Increase the heat to high. Add the bean sprouts, softened rice sticks, light soy sauce, and chicken stock to the wok and stir to mix them with the other ingredients. Stir-fry until the ingredients are just wilted, 2–3 minutes.

3 Add the peeled shrimp to the wok and stir-fry until they just turn pink, 1–1½ minutes.

5 Add the eggs to the other ingredients and stir until they are thoroughly mixed and very hot, about 1 minute. Taste and add more soy sauce, if necessary.

TO SERVE
Transfer the fried rice noodles to warmed individual plates, sprinkle with the scallions, and serve at once.

VARIATION
THAI FRIED NOODLES
PAD THAI
This is Thailand's most famous noodle dish, enjoyed morning, noon, and night. You'll find numerous versions among sidewalk vendors, restaurants, and home cooks.

1 Omit the sausages, onions, soy sauce, and stock. Use ¼-inch rice sticks; soak and drain as directed.
2 Put 2 tbsp dried shrimp in a small bowl and cover with boiling water. Let soak, 30 minutes.
3 Combine 1 tbsp tamarind pulp and 3–4 tbsp boiling water in a bowl; stir with chopsticks to dissolve the pulp.

Rice noodles are a traditional partner for shrimp, sausage, and vegetables

4 Strain the tamarind pulp to extract 2 tbsp thick tamarind water. (You can substitute 1 tbsp lemon juice and 1 tbsp water.) In a bowl, combine the tamarind water with 3 tbsp fish sauce and 1 tbsp sugar. Stir to mix well.
5 Prepare the remaining ingredients as directed, cutting the scallions into 1-inch lengths. In a mortar, grind the garlic and chili peppers together with a pestle to form a paste. Alternatively, chop the ingredients as finely as possible to form a paste. Drain the rice sticks as directed. Drain the dried shrimp and pat dry with paper towels. Finely chop the shrimp.
6 Heat the wok, cook the eggs as directed, and remove them. Increase the heat and add the oil. When hot, add the garlic-chili paste, and dried shrimp; stir-fry until fragrant, about 15 seconds. Add the fresh shrimp and stir-fry as directed.
7 Add the softened rice sticks and tamarind mixture; stir-fry until they are transparent, 3–4 minutes. Reduce the heat to medium.
8 Add the eggs, scallions, and three-quarters of the bean sprouts and stir-fry, about 1 minute longer. Transfer to warmed individual plates. Sprinkle each with 1 tbsp chopped unsalted roasted peanuts. Garnish with the remaining sprouts, a lime wedge, and a sprig of fresh coriander (cilantro).

MIXED PICKLED VEGETABLES

Acar

🍴 SERVES 8–10   🥣 WORK TIME 35–45 MINUTES*   🍲 COOKING TIME ABOUT 10 MINUTES

EQUIPMENT

large bowl

wok

cleaver †

colander

mortar and pestle ‡

wok spatula

vegetable peeler

chopping board

rubber gloves

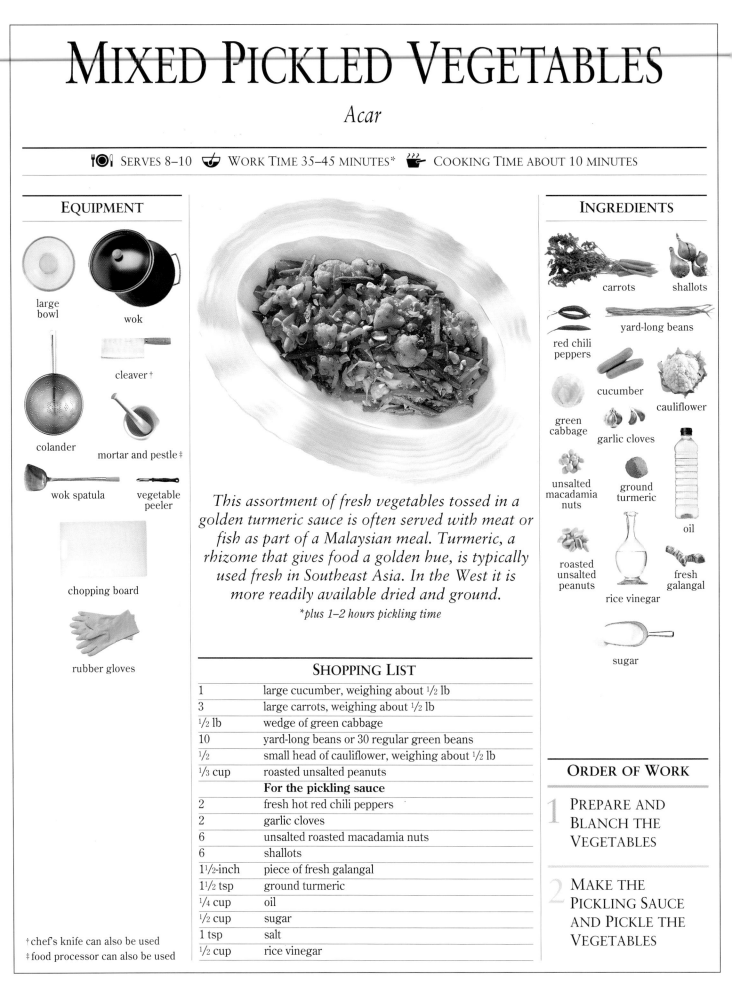

This assortment of fresh vegetables tossed in a golden turmeric sauce is often served with meat or fish as part of a Malaysian meal. Turmeric, a rhizome that gives food a golden hue, is typically used fresh in Southeast Asia. In the West it is more readily available dried and ground.

*plus 1–2 hours pickling time

INGREDIENTS

carrots

shallots

red chili peppers

yard-long beans

cucumber

cauliflower

green cabbage

garlic cloves

unsalted macadamia nuts

ground turmeric

oil

roasted unsalted peanuts

rice vinegar

fresh galangal

sugar

SHOPPING LIST

1	large cucumber, weighing about ½ lb
3	large carrots, weighing about ½ lb
½ lb	wedge of green cabbage
10	yard-long beans or 30 regular green beans
½	small head of cauliflower, weighing about ½ lb
⅓ cup	roasted unsalted peanuts
	For the pickling sauce
2	fresh hot red chili peppers
2	garlic cloves
6	unsalted roasted macadamia nuts
6	shallots
1½-inch	piece of fresh galangal
1½ tsp	ground turmeric
¼ cup	oil
½ cup	sugar
1 tsp	salt
½ cup	rice vinegar

ORDER OF WORK

1 PREPARE AND BLANCH THE VEGETABLES

2 MAKE THE PICKLING SAUCE AND PICKLE THE VEGETABLES

† chef's knife can also be used
‡ food processor can also be used

1 PREPARE AND BLANCH THE VEGETABLES

1 Peel and trim the cucumber, then cut it lengthwise in half. Scoop out the seeds from each half with your thumb and discard them.

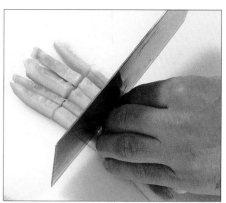

2 Cut the cucumber halves lengthwise into ¼-inch strips, then gather the strips into a bundle and cut them into 2-inch sticks.

3 Peel and trim the carrots, then cut each one crosswise into 3-inch pieces. Cut each piece lengthwise into ¼-inch slices. Stack the slices and cut each stack lengthwise into ¼-inch sticks.

Carrot is indispensable for adding color _____

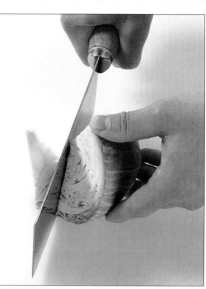

4 Resting the stem end on the chopping board, cut out the core from the wedge of cabbage; discard it.

Yard-long beans, a favorite Asian ingredient, are sometimes called asparagus beans

5 Set the cabbage, cut-side down, on the chopping board and finely shred it. Discard any thick ribs.

6 Trim the yard-long beans and cut them diagonally into 2-inch pieces. If using regular green beans, snap off the ends, pulling away any strings from each side before cutting.

7 Using the cleaver, trim the florets from the head of cauliflower, cutting or pulling them in half if they are large. Discard the core.

Simmer vegetables in water to soften them slightly

8 Fill the wok with water to a depth of 2 inches, and bring to a boil. Add the prepared carrots, cauliflower, and beans.

! TAKE CARE !
If using a round-bottomed wok, place it on a wok ring for stability when boiling.

9 Simmer the vegetables until tender but still crisp, 2–3 minutes, then add the cucumber and cabbage, and simmer, about 1 minute longer.

10 Drain the vegetables in the colander. Rinse with cold water, and drain again thoroughly, tossing gently to eliminate any water.

2 MAKE THE PICKLING SAUCE AND PICKLE THE VEGETABLES

Chili pepper adds heat to pickling sauce

1 Wearing rubber gloves, cut the chili peppers lengthwise in half; discard the cores. Scrape out the seeds and cut away the fleshy white ribs. Cut each half into very thin strips. Gather the strips and cut across into very fine dice.

! TAKE CARE !
Wear rubber gloves when preparing fresh chili peppers, since they can burn your skin.

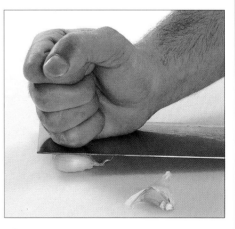

2 Set the flat side of the cleaver on top of each garlic clove and strike it with your fist. Discard the skin and finely chop the garlic.

How to Dice Shallots

If the large blade of the cleaver seems unwieldy when dicing shallots, you can use a regular knife instead.

1 Peel the outer papery skin from each shallot. (If necessary, separate the shallot into sections at the root and peel the sections.) Cut rounded shallots in half.

Shallots may be made up of one or two sections

Cut shallots in half so they sit flat for chopping

2 Set each shallot section or shallot half, flat-side down, on a chopping board and slice horizontally, leaving the slices attached at the root end.

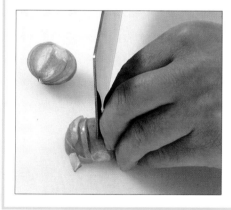

3 Slice vertically through the shallot toward the root end, again leaving the root end uncut.

4 Cut across the shallot to make dice. Continue chopping until very fine.

3 Finely chop the macadamia nuts with the cleaver. Dice the shallots (see box, above), and finely chop the galangal (see box, page 94).

ANNE SAYS
"Asians use native kemiri *nuts, often called candlenuts. Macadamias have a similar rich flavor and texture."*

Finely chopped chili peppers will blend into pounded mixture

4 In the mortar, pound the garlic, nuts, shallots, galangal, turmeric, and chili peppers with the pestle, adding one ingredient at a time and pounding well after each addition.

ANNE SAYS
"Alternatively, work the ingredients to a paste in a food processor, in which case you need only peel the vegetables, and not finely chop them."

Chili-nut paste with sugar and vinegar is hot, sweet, and sour

5 Heat the wok over medium heat until hot. Drizzle in the oil to coat the sides and bottom of the wok. Continue heating until the oil is hot, then add the chili-nut paste and cook, stirring, until slightly thickened and the spices are fragrant, 3–5 minutes.

6 Stir in the sugar, salt, and vinegar; bring to a boil. Remove the wok from the heat.

HOW TO PEEL, SLICE, AND CHOP GALANGAL

Galangal is a gingerlike rhizome with a distinct earthy aroma and spicy flavor. Its texture is very fibrous, so it must be finely chopped before use.

1 With the cleaver, trim any stems or knobs from the galangal and scrape off the skin.

2 Cut the galangal into thin slices, cutting across the fibrous grain.

Crush galangal to soften its fibrous texture

3 Place the flat side of the cleaver on top of each slice and strike it with your fist.

4 With the cleaver, chop the crushed slices of galangal until they become quite fine.

Vegetables should remain firm

VARIATION

VEGETABLE AND TOFU SALAD IN PEANUT SAUCE

This variation of Acar borrows the vegetables and tofu from classic Indonesian gado gado *for a more complete meal.*

7 Add the prepared vegetables to the pickling sauce in the wok and toss to coat them thoroughly. Taste for seasoning, adding more salt if needed.

8 Transfer the warm vegetables to the bowl, and cover tightly. Let stand, about 1 hour at room temperature or at least 2 hours in the refrigerator. Meanwhile, coarsely chop the peanuts with the cleaver.

🍴 **TO SERVE**
Mound the vegetables in a serving dish and sprinkle with the coarsely chopped peanuts. Serve slightly chilled or at room temperature.

Chilled Acar makes a delicious salad or side dish – colorful, crisp, and spicy

Pickled cauliflower is golden with turmeric

1 Omit the cabbage, cauliflower, peanuts, and pickling sauce. Blanch the cucumber, carrots, and beans as directed.
2 Pick over 3 cups (about ½ lb) bean sprouts, discarding any that are discolored. Remove the fine roots and green hulls, then rinse the sprouts under water, and drain.
3 Rinse and drain ½ lb firm tofu. Half-fill a pan with water and bring to a boil. Add the tofu and simmer, turning once, about 10 minutes. Drain and cool on paper towels, and cut into ½-inch cubes.
4 Make a peanut sauce: chop 6 shallots, 2 garlic cloves, and 2 chili peppers as directed. Work to a paste with 1 cup chopped roasted unsalted peanuts, using a mortar and pestle or food processor. Finish the sauce as directed, using 2 tbsp sugar, ¼ cup rice vinegar, ¼ cup water, the juice of 1 lime, and 1 tbsp soy sauce.
5 Arrange the bean sprouts on individual plates and top with the carrots, beans, cucumber, and tofu. Spoon some sauce over the salad. Cover, and refrigerate, about 1 hour.

--- **GETTING AHEAD** ---
The pickled vegetables can be prepared 2–3 days ahead and kept, covered, in the refrigerator.

INDONESIAN FRIED RICE

Nasi Goreng

🍽 SERVES 4   🥣 WORK TIME 40–45 MINUTES*   🍲 COOKING TIME 10–15 MINUTES

EQUIPMENT

strainer

wok, with lid

paper towels

tray

chopsticks

small knife

bowls

medium saucepan, with lid

mortar and pestle†

wok spatula

chef's knife‡

chopping board

† food processor can also be used

‡ cleaver can also be used

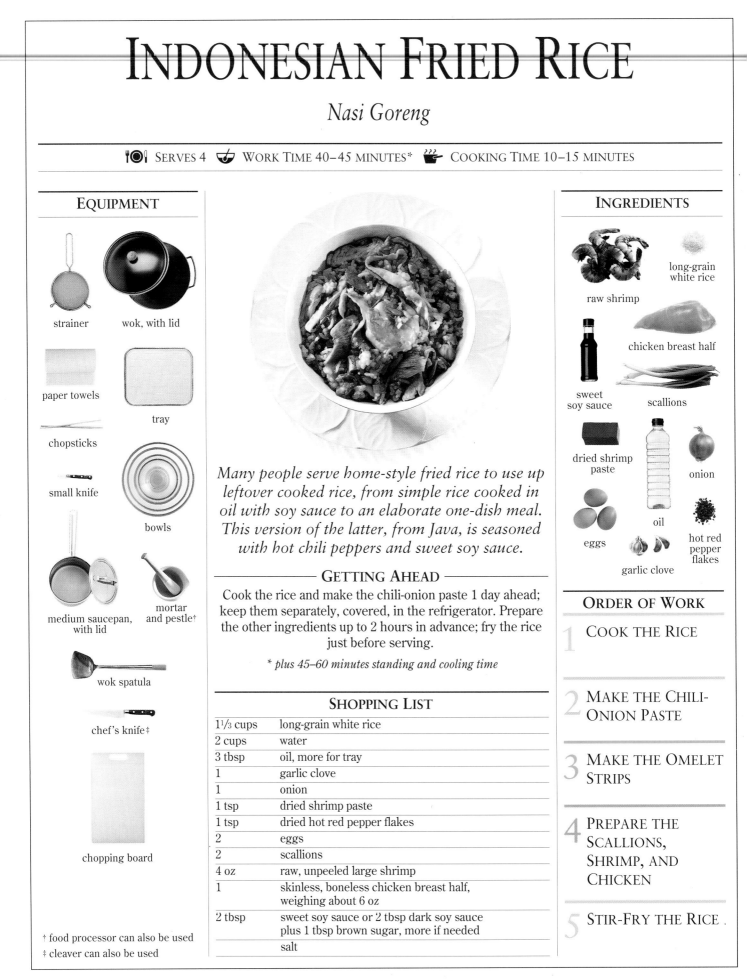

Many people serve home-style fried rice to use up leftover cooked rice, from simple rice cooked in oil with soy sauce to an elaborate one-dish meal. This version of the latter, from Java, is seasoned with hot chili peppers and sweet soy sauce.

GETTING AHEAD

Cook the rice and make the chili-onion paste 1 day ahead; keep them separately, covered, in the refrigerator. Prepare the other ingredients up to 2 hours in advance; fry the rice just before serving.

* plus 45–60 minutes standing and cooling time

SHOPPING LIST

1⅓ cups	long-grain white rice
2 cups	water
3 tbsp	oil, more for tray
1	garlic clove
1	onion
1 tsp	dried shrimp paste
1 tsp	dried hot red pepper flakes
2	eggs
2	scallions
4 oz	raw, unpeeled large shrimp
1	skinless, boneless chicken breast half, weighing about 6 oz
2 tbsp	sweet soy sauce or 2 tbsp dark soy sauce plus 1 tbsp brown sugar, more if needed
	salt

INGREDIENTS

raw shrimp

long-grain white rice

chicken breast half

sweet soy sauce

scallions

dried shrimp paste

onion

oil

eggs

hot red pepper flakes

garlic clove

ORDER OF WORK

1 **COOK THE RICE**

2 **MAKE THE CHILI-ONION PASTE**

3 **MAKE THE OMELET STRIPS**

4 **PREPARE THE SCALLIONS, SHRIMP, AND CHICKEN**

5 **STIR-FRY THE RICE**

1 COOK THE RICE

1 Put the rice in a bowl, cover with cold water, and stir with your fingertips until the water is milky-white. Pour off the water. Repeat once or twice until the water is fairly clear. Drain the rice in the strainer.

2 Put the drained rice in the saucepan and add the measured water. Bring to a boil over high heat. Stir the rice with the chopsticks. Cover the pan, reduce the heat to low, and simmer until all the water has been absorbed and the rice is tender, about 15 minutes.

Chopsticks fluff grains of cooked rice without crushing them

3 Remove from the heat and let the rice stand, without lifting the lid, 15 minutes. Uncover, and stir the rice with the chopsticks to fluff it.

4 Lightly oil the tray, using your fingers. Transfer the rice to the tray, and spread out evenly with your oiled fingers. Let the rice cool to room temperature, 30–45 minutes. Meanwhile, make the chili-onion paste and the omelet strips, and prepare the remaining ingredients.

2 MAKE THE CHILI-ONION PASTE

1 Set the flat side of the chef's knife on top of the garlic clove and strike it with your fist. Discard the skin and coarsely chop the garlic.

2 Peel the onion and trim the top; leave a little of the root attached to hold it together. Finely chop the onion (see box, page 98).

Papery onion skin is scraped off with knife

HOW TO CHOP AN ONION

Chop an onion efficiently and quickly to avoid irritating your eyes.

1 Cut the onion lengthwise in half. Place one half cut-side down. Hold it steady with one hand. Make a series of horizontal cuts from the top toward the root, but not through it.

ANNE SAYS
"The size of the onion dice depends on the thickness of the initial slices."

2 Make a series of lengthwise vertical cuts, cutting just to the root but not through it.

3 Slice the onion crosswise to obtain dice. Repeat for the other half. Continue chopping until you have the fineness required

3 In the mortar, pound the chopped onion with the pestle until pulpy. Add the garlic, shrimp paste, and red pepper flakes and pound until the mixture forms a coarse paste. Alternatively, purée the ingredients in the food processor. Set the paste aside.

3 MAKE THE OMELET STRIPS

1 Beat the eggs in a small bowl with the chopsticks. Heat the wok over medium heat until hot.

2 Drizzle in 1 tbsp of the oil to coat the bottom and sides of the wok. Continue heating until the oil is hot, then pour in the beaten eggs.

Add egg quickly to hot wok

3 Quickly tilt the wok so that the egg spreads over the bottom in an even layer about 1/8-inch thick. Cook until the thin omelet is set in the center and appears slightly crisp around the edge, 1–2 minutes.

! TAKE CARE !
Do not spread the egg too thinly or it may tear when turning the omelet.

Swirl egg to form even coating

4 With the wok spatula, lift the omelet and turn it over. Cook until the other side is lightly browned, 15–30 seconds longer.

Roll omelet loosely so it does not stick

5 Slide the omelet out of the wok onto the chopping board. Let cool slightly. Roll up the omelet loosely. With the chef's knife, cut the omelet across into 1/4- to 1/2-inch strips.

4 PREPARE THE SCALLIONS, SHRIMP, AND CHICKEN

1 Trim the scallions and cut them diagonally into 1/4-inch slices, including some of their green tops.

2 Peel the shells from the shrimp with your fingers.

Shrimp shell comes off easily in your fingers

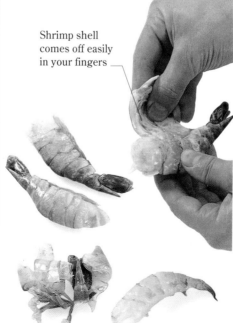

3 Make a shallow cut along the back of each shrimp with the small knife and remove the dark intestinal vein. Rinse the shrimp and pat them dry with paper towels.

4 Separate the small piece of fillet meat from the chicken breast by pulling it off with your fingers. Strip the tendon from the fillet, stroking it with the knife to remove it cleanly, then cut the fillet into thin slices.

5 Holding your hand firmly on top of the chicken breast, cut the meat diagonally into very thin slices.

5 STIR-FRY THE RICE

1 Heat the wok over medium-high heat. Drizzle in 1 tbsp oil to coat the bottom and sides. When oil is hot, add the chili-onion paste; cook, stirring, until fragrant, about 30 seconds.

2 Increase the heat to high. Add the chicken slices and stir-fry until they are opaque, 2–3 minutes.

3 Add the shrimp and stir-fry until they turn pink, about 1–2 minutes. Using the spatula, transfer the chicken and shrimp from the wok to a bowl and keep warm.

4 Reduce the heat to medium. Heat the remaining oil in the wok. Add the cooled rice and stir-fry until each grain is separate, 1–2 minutes. Cover and cook the rice until it softens, about 3 minutes, stirring twice to prevent it from browning.

ANNE SAYS
"For successful fried rice, the rice must be cold or at least at room temperature. If warm, it will be too soft to fry."

Sweet soy sauce flavors and colors rice

Scallions soften during stir-frying but still add crunch

5 Add the scallion slices, sweet soy sauce, and a little salt and stir-fry, about 1 minute longer.

6 Return the omelet strips, chicken, and shrimp to the wok; stir-fry with the rice over high heat until thoroughly combined and very hot, 2–3 minutes. Taste for seasoning, adding more soy sauce, if needed.

¡◎¡ TO SERVE

Transfer the rice to warmed individual bowls, and serve at once.

Chicken, shrimp, and omelet strips make this a substantial dish

VARIATION

THAI CURRY FRIED RICE

KAO PAD

Fragrant with curry spices and garlic, this is a very popular Thai dish.

1 Omit the shrimp paste, hot red pepper flakes, shrimp, and sweet soy sauce. Cook and cool the rice as directed.

2 Prepare the garlic, onion, and scallions as directed. Do not pound the onion and garlic to a paste. Beat the eggs as directed.

3 Cut $3/4$ lb skinless boneless chicken breasts into $3/4$-inch cubes. Core and seed $1/2$ red bell pepper and cut into thin strips.

4 Heat the wok over high heat and drizzle in 2 tbsp oil. When hot, add the onion and pepper, and stir-fry, about 1 minute. Add the chicken, garlic, 1 tbsp curry powder, 1 tsp ground coriander, and 1 tsp ground cumin and stir-fry, 2–3 minutes. Add the rice, 2 tbsp fish sauce, and a little salt; stir-fry until mixed. Reduce the heat to medium, cover, and cook until the rice softens, about 3 minutes, stirring twice during cooking.

5 Make a well in the rice, add the remaining 1 tbsp oil, and heat until hot. Add the eggs; cook until the bottom is set, about 1 minute. Stir to break up the eggs, then stir into the rice.

6 Transfer the rice to warmed individual bowls, sprinkle with the scallions, and serve very hot.

Buddha's Delight

Lo Han Chai

🍽 SERVES 4 🥣 WORK TIME 40–50 MINUTES* 🍲 COOKING TIME 15–20 MINUTES

EQUIPMENT

cleaver†

wok

bowls

chopsticks

small knife

wok spatula

slotted spoon

paper towels

colander

chopping board

strainer

†chef's knife can also be used

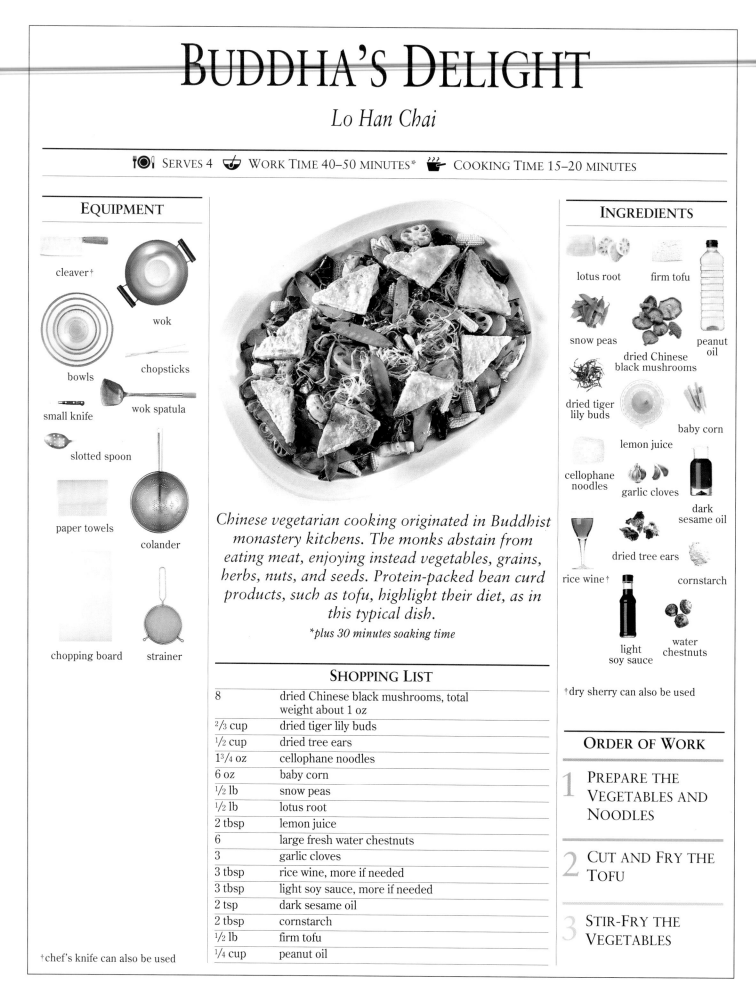

Chinese vegetarian cooking originated in Buddhist monastery kitchens. The monks abstain from eating meat, enjoying instead vegetables, grains, herbs, nuts, and seeds. Protein-packed bean curd products, such as tofu, highlight their diet, as in this typical dish.

*plus 30 minutes soaking time

SHOPPING LIST

8	dried Chinese black mushrooms, total weight about 1 oz
²/₃ cup	dried tiger lily buds
¹/₂ cup	dried tree ears
1³/₄ oz	cellophane noodles
6 oz	baby corn
¹/₂ lb	snow peas
¹/₂ lb	lotus root
2 tbsp	lemon juice
6	large fresh water chestnuts
3	garlic cloves
3 tbsp	rice wine, more if needed
3 tbsp	light soy sauce, more if needed
2 tsp	dark sesame oil
2 tbsp	cornstarch
¹/₂ lb	firm tofu
¹/₄ cup	peanut oil

INGREDIENTS

lotus root   firm tofu

snow peas   peanut oil

dried Chinese black mushrooms

dried tiger lily buds

baby corn

lemon juice

cellophane noodles

garlic cloves

dark sesame oil

dried tree ears

rice wine†   cornstarch

light soy sauce   water chestnuts

†dry sherry can also be used

ORDER OF WORK

1 PREPARE THE VEGETABLES AND NOODLES

2 CUT AND FRY THE TOFU

3 STIR-FRY THE VEGETABLES

1 PREPARE THE VEGETABLES AND NOODLES

1 Put the black mushrooms, tiger lily buds, and tree ears in separate bowls. Add enough warm water to each bowl to cover, and let soak, about 30 minutes.

2 Put the cellophane noodles in a bowl and cover with warm water. Let soak until soft, about 30 minutes.

Kernels and cob of baby corn are both edible

Baby corn looks more attractive when cut on the diagonal

3 Trim the baby corn and cut each ear diagonally in half.

4 Trim the end from each snow pea and pull the string down the pod. Repeat at the other end, pulling the string from the other side.

ANNE SAYS
"If snow peas are young, they will not have strings, so just trim the ends."

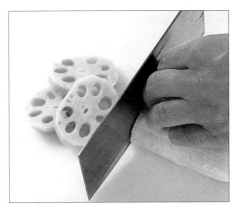

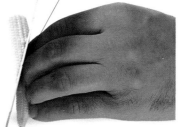

Fresh water chestnuts should be hard and crisp

5 With the cleaver, scrape the skin from the lotus root and slice across into 1/2-inch rounds. Put the lotus root and the lemon juice in a bowl of cold water to prevent the lotus root from discoloring.

6 With the small knife, cut away the peel from the water chestnuts, dropping them into a bowl of cold water as you work. Remove them from the water, slice across into rounds, then return the slices to the water.

7 Peel and chop the garlic (see box, right). Drain the tiger lily buds and tree ears and rinse well with water to remove any grit. Drain, and squeeze them dry.

Tree ears have little taste, but are used for their rich color and chewy texture

8 Cut off and discard the tough ends of the tiger lily buds and the tree ears. If the tree ears are large, cut them into 2-inch pieces.

9 Drain the cellophane noodles in the colander, place them on the chopping board, and cut them into 4- to 5-inch lengths.

10 Drain the black mushrooms, reserving the liquid. Trim off the woody stems, then slice the mushroom caps.

HOW TO PEEL AND CHOP GARLIC

The strength of garlic varies with age; use more when very fresh.

1 Set the flat side of a cleaver on top of the garlic clove and strike it firmly with your fist. Peel off the skin from the garlic clove with your fingers and discard it.

2 Finely chop the garlic, using the cleaver, moving the blade back and forth.

11 Line the strainer with paper towels and set it over a measuring cup. Strain ³/₄ cup of the mushroom soaking liquid into the measuring cup; discard the remainder.

Strain mushroom soaking liquid to remove any sand

12 In a bowl, combine the mushroom liquid, rice wine, soy sauce, sesame oil, and half of the cornstarch, and stir until smooth.

2 CUT AND FRY THE TOFU

1 Rinse the tofu under cold running water and drain it well. Pat dry, using paper towels.

2 Set the tofu on the chopping board and cut it diagonally twice from corner to corner to make 4 triangles.

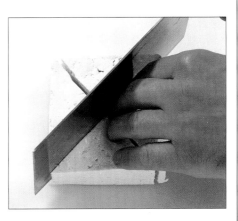

3 Cut each tofu triangle horizontally in half to make 8 triangles. Pat the tofu triangles dry on more paper towels.

ANNE SAYS
"Tofu comes in many shapes. For this recipe, cut the tofu as necessary to create 8 triangles that are about ¹/₂-inch thick."

Coat tofu evenly with cornstarch

Cornstarch will give tofu crispness when fried

4 Put the remaining cornstarch on a plate. Dip the tofu triangles into the cornstarch, patting lightly to coat them evenly.

5 Heat the wok over high heat until very hot. Drizzle in the oil to coat the bottom and sides. Continue heating until the oil is very hot, then add the tofu triangles and fry until they are golden brown, turning with the wok spatula to brown them evenly on all sides, 6–8 minutes.

6 With the wok spatula, transfer the browned tofu triangles to a plate and cover to keep warm. Reduce the heat to medium.

3 STIR-FRY THE VEGETABLES

1 Drain the lotus root and water chestnuts. Add them to the wok with the baby corn, and stir-fry until the lotus root begins to soften, 3–4 minutes.

2 Add the snow peas and garlic to the wok and stir-fry, about 1 minute longer.

Hold wok steady when stir-frying

3 Add the the tiger lily buds, black mushrooms, and tree ears to the wok and stir-fry, about 1 minute.

Tiger lily buds and mushrooms will soften slightly when stir-fried

4 Stir the cornstarch mixture again, then add it to the wok. Bring to a boil, stir-frying constantly until the mixture thickens, 1–2 minutes.

5 Add the softened cellophane noodles and stir-fry until very hot and well mixed with the vegetables, about 2 minutes. Taste for seasoning, adding more rice wine or soy sauce, if needed.

¶☯¶ TO SERVE

Transfer the vegetable and noodle mixture to a warmed serving dish and arrange the tofu triangles on top.

Golden tofu contrasts with crisp vegetables in a combination of flavors and textures

V A R I A T I O N

VIETNAMESE VEGETARIAN STIR-FRY

LA HAN CHAY

This vegetarian dish includes leeks, carrots, and cauliflower that were introduced to Vietnam by European settlers.

1 Omit the tiger lily buds, baby corn, snow peas, lotus root, water chestnuts, garlic, and rice wine. Prepare the Chinese black mushrooms, tree ears, and noodles as directed.

2 Cut ¹/₂ lb yard-long beans or regular green beans diagonally into 2-inch lengths. Trim 1 leek, discarding the root and tough green tops. Slit it lengthwise in half and rinse thoroughly in cold water. Set each half, cut-side down, on a chopping board and cut across into thin slices.

3 Peel 2 small carrots and trim the ends. Cut each carrot diagonally into thin slices. Trim the florets from ¹/₂ small head of cauliflower, cutting large florets in half or into quarters.

4 Heat the oil in the wok as directed. Rinse, drain, and dry the tofu, but do not cut it into triangles. Coat the tofu with 1 tbsp cornstarch, then brown it as directed. Drain the fried tofu on paper towels.

5 Add the leek to the wok and stir-fry until fragrant, about 15 seconds. Add the beans, carrots, and cauliflower and stir-fry, about 1 minute. Add 1 cup bamboo shoots, the Chinese black mushrooms, tree ears, and the ³/₄ cup mushroom liquid. Stir-fry the vegetables until crisp-tender, about 5 minutes.

6 Meanwhile, cut the fried tofu into ¹/₂-inch slices.

7 Stir the soy sauce, sesame oil, 2 tsp sugar, and ¹/₄ tsp ground black pepper into the vegetables. Add the softened noodles and fried tofu, and toss gently until they are hot and coated with the mushroom liquid, about 2 minutes. Taste for seasoning and serve immediately.

GETTING AHEAD

The vegetables and noodles can be prepared up to 1 day ahead and kept, covered, in the refrigerator. Fry the tofu and vegetables just before serving.

ALMOND MILK CURD WITH FRESH FRUIT

Xian Guo Xan Ren Dou Fu

🍽 SERVES 8   🥣 WORK TIME 40 MINUTES*

EQUIPMENT

8-inch square cake pan

saucepans, 1 heavy-based

chopsticks

metal spoon

metal spatula

small knife

bowls

chopping board

ANNE SAYS
"A heavy-based saucepan is essential for cooking the milk and sugar so the mixture does not scorch."

Desserts do not conclude a Chinese meal. Instead, a sweet soup or dessert with fruit is usually served between courses to freshen the palate. This dish, made from sweetened milk and almond extract, resembles bean curd in appearance, but its delicate texture and flavor make it a perfect light dessert in the West.

* plus 3–4 hours chilling time

SHOPPING LIST

4	tangerines
1 lb	lychees
8	sprigs of fresh mint
	For the almond milk curd
2½ cups	milk
⅓ cup	sugar
2 tbsp	powdered unflavored gelatin
½ cup	water
1 tsp	almond extract
	For the sugar syrup
½ cup	water
⅓ cup	sugar

INGREDIENTS

tangerines†   lychees‡

sugar

milk   almond extract

mint

unflavored gelatin

†8-oz can of mandarin oranges, drained, can also be used

‡14-oz can of lychees, drained, can also be used

ORDER OF WORK

1 PREPARE THE ALMOND MILK CURD

2 MAKE THE SYRUP AND PREPARE THE FRUIT

3 FINISH THE DISH

1 PREPARE THE ALMOND MILK CURD

Chopsticks are effective stirring tools

3 Warm the pan over very low heat without stirring, shaking it occasionally, until the gelatin is melted.

1 Combine the milk and sugar in a medium heavy-based saucepan and slowly bring to a boil over medium heat, stirring occasionally with the chopsticks until the sugar has completely dissolved.

2 Sprinkle the gelatin over the water in a small saucepan and let stand until spongy, about 5 minutes.

4 Off the heat, stir the gelatin into the milk mixture, then stir in the almond extract.

5 Pour the almond-flavored mixture into the cake pan. Let cool to room temperature, then cover tightly, and refrigerate until the almond milk curd is set, 3–4 hours.

Mixture will set firmly as soon as it is cold

2 MAKE THE SYRUP AND PREPARE THE FRUIT

1 For the syrup, combine the water and sugar in a small saucepan and heat, stirring occasionally, until the sugar has dissolved.

2 Bring to a boil and simmer the syrup, about 1 minute. Remove from the heat and let cool.

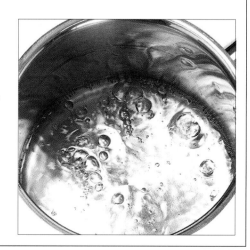

3 With your fingers, peel the skin from the tangerines and separate the sections.

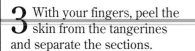

Tangerines are easy to peel, and can be pulled into sections with your fingers

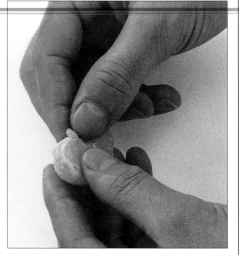

Choose tangerines that are plump and juicy

Rough lychee skin conceals moist pearly interior

4 With your fingers, open the membrane and squeeze the seeds from each tangerine section. Discard the seeds. Put the sections into a large bowl.

5 Peel the lychees with your fingers or the small knife, discarding the stems. Slit the lychee flesh on one side and remove the pit. Add the lychees to the tangerines.

7 Toss gently to coat the fruit. Cover tightly and chill before serving, at least 1 hour.

ANNE SAYS
"*Fresh tangerines may not be in season with fresh lychees, so you may have to use canned tangerines – called mandarin oranges – with fresh lychees, or vice versa. For a light alternative, use fruit canned in its natural juices.*"

6 Pour the cooled sugar syrup over the peeled lychees and tangerine sections in the bowl.

3 FINISH THE DISH

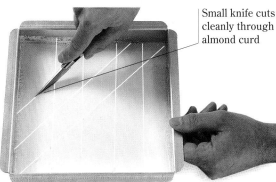

Small knife cuts cleanly through almond curd

1 With the small knife, cut the almond curd into 5 strips about 1½ inches wide; then cut diagonally through the curd from 1 corner to the opposite corner. Make 3 equally spaced cuts on each side of the diagonal to form diamond-shaped pieces. Run the point of the knife around the inside edge of the pan.

2 Spoon the fruit onto individual plates. Loosen the almond curd and carefully lift out the diamonds with the metal spatula.

3 Arrange 2 whole almond curd diamonds, or several pieces, beside the fruit salad.

🍽 TO SERVE
Decorate with the mint sprigs.

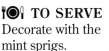

Almond-flavored curd is firm and silky smooth

Lychees are one of China's treasured fruit

ALMOND MILK CURD WITH PLUMS AND ALMONDS

XAN REN DOU FU LIZI XAN REN

The almond milk curd – also called "almond float" – is cut into cubes and served with plums and toasted almonds.

1 Omit the tangerines, lychees, and mint. Prepare the almond milk curd and chill as directed.
2 Prepare 1½ lb fresh plums: cut each in half around the pit. Give a sharp twist to each half to loosen it. Scoop out the pit with the knife. Cut each half into 3 wedges. Make the sugar syrup but do not cool; add the plums. Simmer gently until the plums are just tender, 2–3 minutes. Let cool in the syrup.
3 Heat the oven to 350° F. Spread ½ cup sliced almonds on a baking sheet and toast until lightly browned, 8–10 minutes. Let cool.
4 Cut the almond curd into 9 squares, carefully remove them with the spatula, and set them on a chopping board. Cut each square into 9 cubes. Divide the cubes and the plums and syrup between 8 individual dishes, top with the toasted almonds, and serve.

GETTING AHEAD
The almond milk curd and syrup can be made up to 1 day ahead and kept, covered, in the refrigerator. Cut up the fruit, mix with the syrup, and refrigerate 2–3 hours ahead. Cut the curd just before serving.

BANANA FRITTERS WITH LIME AND CARAMEL SYRUP

Kluay Tord

🍽 SERVES 4   🥣 WORK TIME 15–20 MINUTES*   🍲 COOKING TIME 3–4 MINUTES

EQUIPMENT

citrus juicer

wok

deep-fat thermometer (optional)

chopping board

paper towels

bamboo skimmer†

small knife

medium heavy-based saucepan

medium bowl

cooking chopsticks

chopsticks

† slotted spoon can also be used

ANNE SAYS
"*To test the temperature of the oil without a deep-fat thermometer, drop a cube of bread into the hot oil. If the cube turns golden in about 40 seconds, the oil is ready.*"

In Bangkok, street vendors offer plain bananas coated with a tangy lime syrup, or deep-fried bananas coated with coconut, palm sugar, and crunchy rice. This recipe combines the flavors of these two traditional Thai snacks.

GETTING AHEAD
The syrup can be made up to 1 day ahead and kept, covered, at room temperature. Reheat gently just before using.

* plus 15 minutes standing time

SHOPPING LIST

4	small ripe but firm bananas
	oil for deep-frying
3 tbsp	flour, more if needed
1 cup	unsweetened shredded coconut
	double lime twists (see page 123) for decoration (optional)
	For the batter
½ cup	flour, more if needed
1 tsp	baking soda
½ cup	water, more if needed
1 tbsp	oil
	For the lime and caramel syrup
2	limes
1 cup	light brown sugar
2 tbsp	butter
¼ cup	water

INGREDIENTS

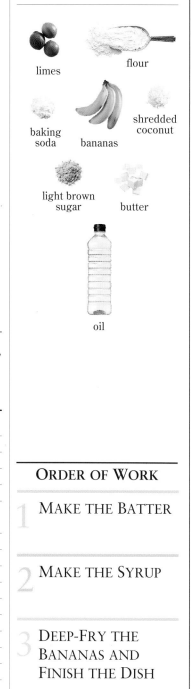

limes

flour

baking soda

bananas

shredded coconut

light brown sugar

butter

oil

ORDER OF WORK

1   MAKE THE BATTER

2   MAKE THE SYRUP

3   DEEP-FRY THE BANANAS AND FINISH THE DISH

1 MAKE THE BATTER

1 Combine the flour and baking soda in the bowl and mix together well with the chopsticks.

Blend dry ingredients with chopsticks

2 Gradually pour the water into the bowl, stirring with the chopsticks, until the batter becomes smooth. Let the batter stand, about 15 minutes. Meanwhile, make the lime and caramel syrup (see below).

3 Add the oil and stir until the batter is smooth. Test with a spoon: it should have the consistency of very thick cream.

ANNE SAYS
"If necessary, add more flour or water to the batter to adjust the consistency."

2 MAKE THE SYRUP

1 Cut the limes in half and squeeze the juice; there should be about 1/3 cup juice.

2 Combine the brown sugar, butter, and water in the saucepan.

Syrup is less likely to scorch in heavy-based pan

Water ensures syrup does not get too thick

3 Bring to a boil over medium heat, stirring until the sugar dissolves. Continue to boil without stirring until slightly thick and syrupy, 2–3 minutes.

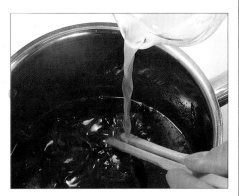

4 Stir 1/4 cup of the lime juice into the syrup until well-mixed. Taste and add more lime juice, if you like. Keep the syrup warm over very low heat.

3 DEEP-FRY THE BANANAS AND FINISH THE DISH

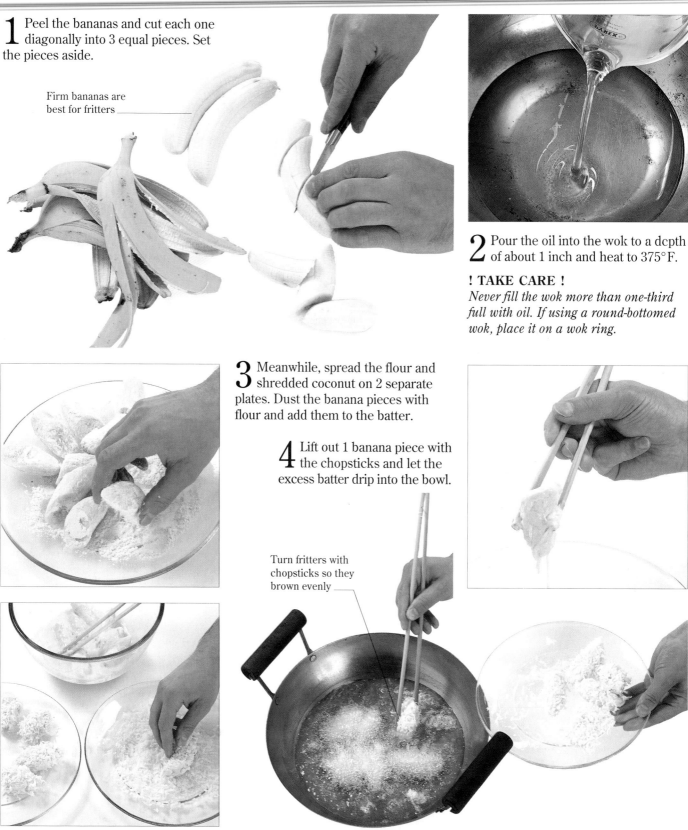

1 Peel the bananas and cut each one diagonally into 3 equal pieces. Set the pieces aside.

Firm bananas are best for fritters

2 Pour the oil into the wok to a depth of about 1 inch and heat to 375°F.

! TAKE CARE !
Never fill the wok more than one-third full with oil. If using a round-bottomed wok, place it on a wok ring.

3 Meanwhile, spread the flour and shredded coconut on 2 separate plates. Dust the banana pieces with flour and add them to the batter.

4 Lift out 1 banana piece with the chopsticks and let the excess batter drip into the bowl.

Turn fritters with chopsticks so they brown evenly

5 With your fingers, roll the banana in the coconut until evenly coated. Transfer to a plate and repeat with the remaining banana pieces.

6 Using the cooking chopsticks, add the banana pieces to the hot oil and deep-fry until golden, turning so the fritters cook evenly, about 1 minute.

ANNE SAYS
"Cooking chopsticks are extra-long. They are useful for deep-frying, because they keep your hands away from the hot fat."

7 Remove the fritters from the wok with the bamboo skimmer, and drain on paper towels.

When brown, lift fritters carefully from oil

8 Carefully spoon a little of the warm lime and caramel syrup onto each of 4 individual dessert plates so that it forms a pool. Arrange 3 banana fritters on each plate.

🍽 TO SERVE
Decorate with double lime twists, if you like, and serve immediately.

Syrup spiked with lime juice complements banana fritters

APPLE FRITTERS WITH CARAMEL SYRUP AND SESAME

In this easy version of a favorite Chinese sweet snack, wedges of apple are coated in batter and deep-fried, then drizzled with a warm caramel syrup, and sprinkled with sesame seeds.

1 Omit the bananas, limes, and coconut. Make the batter as directed.
2 Make the caramel syrup, substituting 1 tbsp lemon juice for all of the lime juice. Keep the syrup warm.
3 Peel 3 medium apples (total weight about 1 lb), and cut out the flower and stem ends. Quarter the apples and cut out the cores. Cut each cored quarter into 2 wedges.
4 Dust the apple wedges with flour, coat them in batter, then deep-fry as directed. Drain the fritters on paper towels, then arrange them on a serving platter, and drizzle with the warm caramel syrup. Sprinkle with 2 tbsp sesame seeds and serve immediately.

STICKY RICE WITH MANGOES

Khao Niew Mamuang

🍽️ SERVES 6   🥣 WORK TIME 40 MINUTES*   ♨️ COOKING TIME 40–50 MINUTES

EQUIPMENT

strainer

wok, with lid

bamboo steamer, with lid †

medium heavy-based saucepan

chef's knife

bowl

small knife

wooden spoon

chopping board

cheesecloth

† metal vegetable steamer can also be used

ANNE SAYS

"*A heavy-based saucepan is used so the coconut milk and sugar do not stick and scorch.*"

INGREDIENTS

sweet rice

mangoes

sugar

coconut milk

This well-known Thai dessert of coconut-flavored rice pudding with slices of ripe, juicy mango provides a tropical ending to any spicy Asian meal. You should use sweet rice, also called glutinous or sticky rice, a starchy variety ideal for making creamy desserts. Sweet rice comes in both short-grain and long-grain varieties. Both are suitable for this recipe. You can reserve about 1/4 cup of the thick "cream" that rises to the top of the coconut milk, then spoon it into the center of the rice to finish the dish, if you like.

GETTING AHEAD

The sticky rice can be made 6–8 hours ahead and kept, covered, at room temperature. Prepare the mangoes just before serving.

*plus at least 3 hours soaking time

SHOPPING LIST

2 cups	sweet rice
1/2 cup	sugar
1/2 tsp	salt
1 1/4 cups	canned coconut milk
3	large, ripe mangoes, total weight about 2 lb

ORDER OF WORK

1. PREPARE AND COOK THE RICE

2. MAKE THE STICKY RICE AND PREPARE THE MANGOES

3. FINISH THE DISH

PREPARE AND COOK THE RICE

1 Put the rice in the bowl and cover with cold water. Cover, and let soak, at least 3 hours or overnight.

2 Pour the soaked and softened rice into the strainer to drain off all the liquid.

Rice grains swell and soften slightly during soaking

3 Rinse the rice thoroughly with cold running water to remove any excess starch.

4 Pour enough water into the wok so that it almost touches the bottom of the steamer basket. Cover the wok and bring the water to a boil.

Spread rice flat to cook evenly

5 Line the bottom and side of the steamer basket with a double thickness of dampened cheesecloth.

6 Tip the soaked and drained rice into the basket, and spread it evenly.

Cheesecloth protects rice during steaming

7 Uncover the wok and place the basket of rice over the boiling water. Cover the basket with its lid. Reduce the heat to medium. Steam the rice until tender, 40–50 minutes. The longer the rice has been soaked, the faster it will cook.

! TAKE CARE !

If using a round-bottomed wok, place it on a wok ring so it does not tip during steaming. When the water is boiling, be sure it does not touch the rice. Also, you may need to add boiling water to the wok during cooking to maintain the original level.

2 MAKE THE STICKY RICE AND PREPARE THE MANGOES

1 In the saucepan, combine the sugar and salt with 1 cup of the coconut milk.

2 Bring slowly to a boil, stirring with the wooden spoon, until the sugar dissolves. Remove the pan from the heat.

Stir coconut milk and sugar constantly to prevent scorching

Coconut milk is thick and silky smooth

3 Remove the hot cooked rice from the cheesecloth and stir it into the coconut mixture. Set aside to cool to room temperature, about 30 minutes. Meanwhile, prepare the mangoes (see box, right).

HOW TO PEEL AND SLICE A MANGO

A mango pit is oval. To find the flat sides, roll the mango on the work surface; it will settle on a flat side.

1 Holding the mango in your hand, cut away the peel with a small knife.

2 With a chef's knife, cut the peeled mango lengthwise on both sides of the pit so the knife just misses the pit. Discard the pit.

3 Put each piece of mango cut-side down on a chopping board and, with a chef's knife, cut it lengthwise into 1/4-inch slices.

3 FINISH THE DISH

1 Mound the sticky rice in the center of a serving dish, and arrange the slices of mango around it in a neat, overlapping pattern.

2 With the back of a spoon, make a well in the center of the rice mound. Spoon the remaining ¼ cup coconut milk into the well in the center.

🍽 TO SERVE

Decorate the sticky rice with a few more mango slices, and serve at room temperature.

Ripe mango slices complement the sticky rice perfectly

Coconut "cream" is rich finishing touch

VARIATION

STICKY RICE WITH FRESH PINEAPPLE AND COCONUT

The bright acidity of fresh pineapple is a perfect foil for creamy coconut, with toasted coconut added for crunch.

1 Make the sticky rice as directed in the main recipe. A short while before serving, heat the oven to 375°F. Spread ½ cup unsweetened shredded coconut on a baking sheet and toast in the oven, stirring occasionally so it browns evenly, about 5 minutes. Remove from the oven, and let cool.

2 Cut off the plume and base of a small pineapple (about 2 lb), then peel it with a chef's knife. Work from top to bottom, following the curve of the fruit and cutting deeply enough to remove the eyes with the pineapple skin.

3 Cut the pineapple lengthwise in half and then into quarters. If the core is not tender, cut it from each quarter and discard it. Cut the quarters crosswise into neat slices.

4 Arrange the sticky rice in small mounds among 6 dessert plates. Make a well in the center of each mound and add a spoonful of the remaining coconut milk. Arrange the pineapple slices around the rice and sprinkle with the toasted coconut.

119

ASIAN KNOW-HOW

EQUIPMENT

The equipment required for Asian cooking is generally simple and inexpensive, although some pieces may not be familiar to the Western cook. Because these tools have been used for centuries, they are efficient and versatile. Just a few perform a wide range of culinary tasks, although some dishes require more specialized items.

While the term *wok* applies specifically to a Chinese cooking vessel, most Asian cooks use a version of this all-purpose pan. The wok and its cousins are bowl-shaped, with gently sloping sides and a wide circumference. They may have ear-shaped handles of metal or wood, a single long handle, or both. Traditional woks are round-based, designed to sit directly on the heat, but flat-based models are now available for use on electric stovetops. A 14-inch wok is a good size – large enough for most recipes, but not so large as to be unwieldy or monopolize the cooking surface.

Heavy-gauge spun steel is the least expensive and perhaps the best material for woks, because it is heavy enough to prevent the ingredients from burning but light enough to maneuver. Cast iron is excellent as well, since it is a good conductor of heat. Both metals will develop a "non-stick" patina with use. Woks already lined with non-stick finishes are not advisable, since they do not let ingredients brown properly and cannot withstand the high heat required for wok cooking. After use, all woks should be wiped out, rinsed with warm water, and dried thoroughly. To season a new wok, scour it clean, then heat it directly over high heat until very hot. Using paper towels, rub the entire inside of the wok with fresh corn or peanut oil. The oil will smoke and the center of the wok will darken. Remove from the heat, rub off excess oil, and let cool, at least 10 minutes. Repeat the process.

Once introduced to wok cooking, many cooks become devoted, leaving their saucepans, frying, and sauté pans on the shelf and making the most of the wok's versatility for a multitude of functions. Stir-frying is the most obvious use for a wok – the wide central area and sloping sides heat quickly and uniformly, and ingredients are easily tossed for even cooking. The wok's large capacity makes it excellent for deep-frying, steaming, or boiling, although you must take care to keep it steady during these operations, especially when using a round-based model. A wok ring provides greater stability.

The cleaver of various weights and sizes is the all-purpose cutting tool in Asian kitchens. The characteristic deep rigid blade attached to a sturdy wooden handle provides excellent balance for tasks from chopping bones to precision cutting, such as deveining shrimp. You can use the end of the cleaver handle with a sturdy bowl as an "instant" mortar and pestle for pounding and crushing. The Japanese use cleavers less than other Asian cooks, preferring slim-bladed knives similar to Western chef's or paring knives.

In your own kitchen, cleavers and Western knives are interchangeable – most important is that you feel comfortable and secure while working. As with any knife, a cleaver should be washed and stored with care, and sharpened frequently. Asian cooks often use the unglazed underside of a ceramic bowl as a whetstone for sharpening.

A heavy mortar and pestle is useful for making the spice pastes of Indonesian and Thai cuisines, and for crushing nuts, seeds, and whole spices. The pestle crushes and smears the ingredients against the rough surface of the mortar's interior. Often a food processor or blender can be substituted.

A familiar symbol of Asian cooking, chopsticks allow dextrous handling of ingredients both in the kitchen and at the table. Keep a pair of simple bamboo chopsticks on hand for stirring, fluffing cooked rice, separating noodles while boiling, and turning or transferring items. Longer sturdier chopsticks are used for deep-frying; their extra length keeps your hands safely away from the sputtering hot fat.

Sometimes, more specialized pieces of equipment are required to create truly authentic Asian dishes, although in most cases an adequate substitute may be found in a Western kitchen.

TECHNIQUES

The range and diversity of dishes in the Asian repertoire is amazing, yet most are easy and quick to prepare. Perhaps the epitome of Asian cooking methods is stir-frying – a quick technique that retains the fresh flavor, color, and texture of the ingredients. To stir-fry, heat the empty wok, then drizzle a small amount of oil around the perimeter so it coats the bottom and sides in a thin layer. Wait a few seconds until the oil is hot before adding the ingredients, this prevents sticking and ensures successful browning. Ingredients should be added in a specific order: usually aromatics first (garlic, ginger, scallions), followed by ingredients needing longer cooking (dense vegetables or meat), then the quicker cooking items. Immediately stir and toss the ingredients with a wok spatula around the entire surface of the wok. Heat is most intense at the center of the wok, with the sides a degree cooler. Often liquid is added toward the end of stir-frying, perhaps a combination of soy sauce, chicken stock, and fish sauce, with a little cornstarch so the mixture thickens and glazes the main ingredients.

Steaming is a widely used Asian technique, increasingly popular with today's health-conscious cooks. Whole fish, such as the red snapper in Steamed Fish in Black Bean Sauce, are appropriate for steaming, as well as small items, like the Steamed Open-Faced Dumplings. Even rice can be steamed; the steamer basket is lined with damp cheesecloth.

Pickling has been used in Asia for centuries to preserve food in hot climates. Two methods appear in this volume: in Mixed Pickled Vegetables, a variety of fresh vegetables are blanched, then tossed in a sweet-sour macadamia nut sauce. A more piquant pickle (*kimchee*) accompanies Korean Grilled Beef: Napa cabbage leaves are soaked in brine, then packed with a fiery daikon and chili pepper mixture and left for several days to ferment until tangy and sour.

Some Asian specialty dishes are only briefly cooked or not cooked at all, allowing fresh clean flavors to come to the fore. In *sushi,* strips of the freshest raw tuna and cucumber are encased in vinegared rice and roasted seaweed, while in Vietnamese spring rolls, cooked shrimp and pork are teamed with crunchy raw vegetables and herbs, all rolled together in softened rice-paper wrappers.

Once you reach a certain level of competence, you can perform a wide range of functions quickly and neatly with a cleaver. You can cut through tough bones neatly with a swift whack from the cleaver, using the force of your shoulder and elbow. Perform finer work with finesse, choking up on the cleaver handle and resting your first two fingers on one side of the blade and your thumb on the other. The flat of the cleaver blade is ideal for crushing garlic, ginger, lemon grass, and galangal to make chopping easier.

A variety of cutting techniques are illustrated in this volume, using both the cleaver and the chef's knife, including finely chopping garlic, ginger, and galangal, slicing beef and chicken, chopping raw beef until minced, boning chicken thighs, and dicing hot chili peppers. Shrimp are deveined and butterflied, or cut into "flowers" for Japanese specialties.

Other Asian techniques presented in this volume include making Chinese pancakes to spread with hoisin sauce and wrap around a stir-fried filling; shaping stuffed dumplings to steam-fry until tender with a crunchy bottom; making spice pastes; drying and roasting a duck to produce a crisp, mahogany-brown skin; and making Japanese soup stock (*dashi*), subtly flavored with a hint of the sea.

INGREDIENTS

In Asian cooking you will find a myriad of ingredients, some familiar to the Western cook, others with exotic appearances and flavors, that may soon become staples in your home because they are so delicious. Impeccable freshness is the hallmark of all Asian cooking.

A visit to an Asian market, its stalls laden with gleaming vegetables, succulent ripe fruit, and bunches of fragrant herbs, reveals this insistence on superior ingredients. In some Asian markets, live fish are displayed in tanks, to be selected by the shopper, then killed and cleaned only at the moment of purchase.

Fish, meat, and poultry are featured in most Asian dishes, but large quantities of these protein ingredients never dominate an Asian meal, being complemented by plenty of rice, noodles, and vegetables. In fact, rice is so important in many Asian cuisines that in some languages the word for "food" is the same as the word for "rice," while other types of food are described by a term "with the rice." There are many varieties of rice. In this volume we cook long-grain white rice so it is fluffy and tender with each grain separate. Short-grain white rice is boiled, then mixed with sweetened rice vinegar, and fanned until glossy and slightly sticky, to shape into *sushi* rolls or mounds. Sweet rice, also called glutinous or sticky rice, may be short- or long-grained. It is mixed with creamy coconut milk and sugar in the Thai recipe for Sticky Rice with Mangoes.

Noodles appear frequently in Asian dishes in both starring and supporting roles. They may be made from wheat, rice, buckwheat, potato, mung bean, or a starchy root called "devil's tongue." In Malaysian Fried Rice Noodles, wide rice noodles are a mild and chewy foil to the assertive flavors of Chinese sausage and chili peppers. Cellophane noodles, made from mung bean starch, complement dried and fresh vegetables in Buddha's Delight, and shirataki noodles – picturesquely named "white waterfall" – are integral to Japanese One-Pot Meal.

Characteristic Asian flavor comes from the careful combination of many seasonings, both fresh and dried, so that no flavor overwhelms, but each contributes subtly to the overall appeal of the dish.

Asian food gets its savory, salty tastes, in particular from two ingredients that replace ordinary salt both in the kitchen and at the table. Soy sauce is perhaps best-known in the West, but fish sauce, called variously *nam pla, nuoc mam,* or *patis* is used throughout the East. More strongly flavored than soy sauce, with a pronounced fragrance, a few drops of fish sauce in cooked dishes or in sauces such as Vietnamese dipping sauce add an unmistakable sweet-salty note. Dried shrimp, dried shrimp paste, and fermented black beans are other frequently used salty ingredients.

Sesame oil, made from toasted sesame seeds, is used for flavoring, but not for cooking, while sesame seeds and nuts, such as peanuts and macadamia nuts, feature in flavoring pastes and are sprinkled on dishes as a crunchy finishing touch. Neutral-flavored oils are preferred for cooking and should be selected according to their ability to withstand very high temperatures – their "smoke point." Peanut oil is a favorite with Chinese cooks; other good choices are soybean, safflower, and canola oils.

Ginger and a similar rhizome called galangal give piquancy to many Asian dishes, while chili peppers of many varieties add heat and spice. Garlic and members of the onion family are ever-present, and lemon grass, with its heady lemony fragrance, often brightens the dish with a hint of acid. Other acidic flavors come from tamarind, lime juice, or rice vinegar.

Fresh vegetables are selected by the Asian cook as much for their texture as for their flavor. In addition to familiar varieties, exotic vegetables, such as Asian spinach, daikon, and the aptly named yard-long green beans make their appearance in this volume.

Fresh flavor and moist but crunchy texture come from water chestnuts, lotus root, and the ubiquitous bean sprouts. Sprouts are sometimes "tidied up" by removing any roots or hulls; for more rustic preparations, they are simply sorted, rinsed, and drained. Favorite herbs, always used fresh, are coriander, Asian basil, and mint. They may be chopped for inclusion in a cooked dish, but are also used as a salad green or as a cooling accompaniment, and as a garnish or decoration.

Dried ingredients are important in Asian cooking, especially in Chinese dishes. Dried Chinese black mushrooms, dried tree ears (a type of fungus), and dried tiger lily buds add a smoky, woody flavor as well as an agreeable chewiness to dishes such as the stir-fried Yellow Flower Pork.

A glossary is presented on pages 124–125 with descriptions of many more Asian ingredients. All soy sauces are made by the same basic method –brewing soy beans and a roasted grain, often wheat, producing a mellow salty liquid. Chinese soy sauce has two main categories: dark, which is a deep color and not too salty, is used in hearty recipes and as a table-top seasoning; light soy sauce, marginally lighter in color and slightly less salty, is more often used to season delicate foods such as seafood, poultry, and vegetables. The most typical Japanese soy sauce (*shoyu*) has a slightly sweet and delicate flavor. It is roughly equivalent in intensity to light Chinese soy sauce. Another type of soy sauce in Malaysian cooking is sweet soy sauce, also called *ketjap manis.* Slightly syrupy, it is flavored with palm syrup, garlic, star anise, salam leaves (similar to bay leaves), and galangal.

DECORATIONS

The presentation of any Asian dish improves dramatically with a colorful decoration.
I find that fresh fruit and vegetables are often the most eye-catching.
Here are a few decorations most frequently used in Asian cooking.

CHILI FLOWER	DOUBLE LIME TWIST	CUCUMBER FENCE	LIME FLOWER

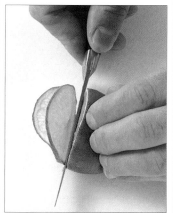

Almost any chili pepper can be transformed into a bright yet delicate flower decoration.

For a nice "twist on the twist," cut a lime slice with 2 layers.

Spiky green "fences" are made from cucumber peel. Cluster several together for best effect.

The bright green peel of a lime wedge is pared and folded under to create a bold floral decoration.

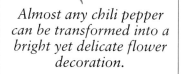

1 Make several lengthwise slits through a chili pepper from below the stem to the pointed end. Wash your hands immediately after handling the chili pepper or wear rubber gloves because the chili pepper can burn your skin.

2 Soak the chili pepper in a bowl of ice water until the ends curl out to form a flower, about 30 minutes. Remove from the water, and pat dry before use.

1 Cut a very thin slice from a lime, but do not completely cut through the base of the slice. Cut a second thin slice, cutting through completely to form a double-layered slice.

2 Slit the slice from the edge to the center and twist to form double curves.

1 Cut a 3-inch piece of cucumber. Carefully pare away the peel with a small knife, keeping it in large pieces.

2 Trim the pared peel to 1½-inch strips and cut out a 3-pointed fence design from each strip.

1 Cut 1 lime lengthwise into 8 wedges. Carefully pare the peel and pith from the flesh, leaving them attached at one end.

2 Fold the peel inward, tucking the end point securely inside to form a leaf-shaped loop.

GLOSSARY

Bamboo shoots: mild flavored, fibrous golden shoots of young bamboo. Used throughout Asia, they are available fresh in spring. Canned bamboo shoots, packed in water, are available sliced, in chunks, or whole.

Basil, Asian: also known as Thai or holy basil. This variety has purplish stems and small serrated-edged leaves with a slightly anise flavor. Regular basil can be substituted.

Bean sauce, ground: a brownish paste made from fermented soybeans. It is used extensively in Chinese and Japanese cooking among others. Sold in jars and cans, it can be kept indefinitely if refrigerated.

Bean sprouts: tender sprouts of green mung beans, not to be confused with soybean sprouts, which have large hard seed heads. Mung bean roots and green hulls are often removed before using.

Beans, black fermented: small black soy beans fermented and preserved with salt and flavorings, used only as a flavoring in Chinese food. Sold in plastic packages. Transfer to a jar and store refrigerated; rinse in water and chop or crush before using.

Beans, yard-long: 18- to 24-inch-long slender beans, also called asparagus beans. Select dark green pods with small beans inside. Regular green beans can also be used.

Bonito flakes, dried: a staple in the Japanese kitchen. Fillet of bonito, a fish in the mackerel family, is dried and shaved into flakes. Used as one of the two essential ingredients of basic soup stock (*dashi*).

Chili peppers, fresh: introduced from the Americas to Southeast Asia by the Portuguese and Dutch in the 15th and 16th centuries. The most readily available variety, used in this volume, is the mildly hot 4- to 5-inch slender green or red variety (red chili peppers are merely ripe green ones). Thai cooks also use tiny 1½- to 2- inch green and red very hot peppers, called bird or Thai chili peppers. The Chinese use whole or flaked dried red chili peppers, while Koreans use red pepper powder.

Coconut milk: the liquid extracted from fresh coconut infused in hot water. Not to be confused with the clear liquid from inside a coconut. If coconut milk is left to stand, the thicker "cream" will rise to the top and can be skimmed off. Canned unsweetened coconut milk can be substituted.

Coriander: also called Chinese parsley or cilantro, the flat leaves have a fragrant aroma and pronounced flavor. The seeds, with a different flavor, are an element of spice blends and pastes.

Daikon: also called *mooli*, a long white radish, used raw in pickles or cooked in soups and stir-fries. A winter radish, it has a crisp texture and peppery flavor.

Fish sauce: also called *nuoc nam* in Vietnam, *nam pla* in Thailand, and *patis* in the Philippines. It is a thin, brown liquid with a pungent aroma extracted from salted fish or shrimp, used for cooking and as a condiment.

Five-spice powder: a Chinese spice blend of ground cloves, cinnamon, fennel, star anise, and Szechwan peppercorns.

Galangal: also called *laos* in Indonesia and *khaa* in Thailand, this rhizome has a musty aroma, pale, lined skin, and a flavor slightly similar to ginger root. It is available fresh or in dried slices.

Hoisin sauce: a slightly sweet, thick, dark brown sauce used in Chinese and Vietnamese cooking as a condiment or barbecue seasoning, made from ground soy beans, garlic, chili peppers, spices, and sweetener.

Kaffir lime leaves: fresh or dried, the aromatic leaves of a Southeast Asian citrus tree. They are used predominantly in Thai cooking and are available fresh or dried.

Konbu: the dried giant sea kelp used for making *dashi*, the traditional Japanese soup stock.

Lemon grass: a long, grass-like herb with a strong lemon flavor and aroma. Only the white bulbous base and part of the stalk are used since the leaves are tough. The peel of regular limes can be substituted.

Lotus root: the underwater root of the lotus plant with lengthwise hollow cavities. It is mild in flavor, with a crunchy texture, and is sold fresh, canned, or dried.

Lychees: small, sweet, fleshy white fruit, with thin brown skin and a large pit. They are available fresh or canned in a sweet syrup.

Maltose: malt sugar, resembling thick honey, used in Chinese cooking for glazing pork and poultry.

Noodles: cellophane noodles, also called transparent noodles, or mung bean threads. Clear, fine dried strands, made from ground mung beans, they are sold in bundles; **thin rice noodles**, also called rice vermicelli and *mai fun* in Chinese, they are wiry white noodles made from rice flour, similar to cellophane noodles; **rice sticks**, flat rice noodles available in different widths from thin, through medium to wide, made from rice flour, water, and salt, sold in folded bundles; **shirataki noodles**, thin transparent gelatinous noodles made from yams, sold packed in water, in refrigerated cases at Japanese markets.

Nori: crisp sheets of seaweed made of *laver*, a sea vegetable, that has been chopped and dried. They are used for wrapping rice into *sushi*. Sold roasted, or plain.

Rice paper: round or triangular brittle translucent sheets made of rice flour, water, and salt; used rehydrated for wrapping fresh or fried spring rolls.

Rice vinegar: clear vinegar made from rice used in cooking and pickling. Japanese rice vinegar is milder than Chinese rice vinegar.

Rice wine: wine made from rice with water. Japnese dry rice wine (*sake*) and Chinese rice wine (*shaoxing*) are used in cooking and for drinking. Japanese sweet rice wine (*mirin*) is used in glazes, salad dressing, and stews.

Sesame oil: strong amber-colored nutty oil extracted from toasted sesame seeds, used for flavoring, not cooking. Do not confuse this dark sesame oil with cold-pressed unroasted sesame oil used for cooking.

Shrimp, dried: peeled tiny whole shrimp that are salted, dried, and used for seasoning soups and stir-fried dishes.

Shrimp paste: a dark odorous paste, made from fermented shrimp, sold as blocks or in jars.

Soy sauce: a major seasoning in Asian cooking, soy is made from fermented soybeans with wheat, yeast, water, salt, and sugar.

Spinach, Asian: similar in flavor to regular spinach, it has short stems and small flat leaves, usually sold with roots attached. Regular spinach can be substituted.

Star anise: this star-shaped dried seed pod of a tree in the magnolia family has a licorice flavor. It is used in braised dishes and soups, and is the major ingredient in Chinese five-spice powder.

Szechwan peppercorns: unrelated to the familiar peppercorns, these are the dried reddish brown berries of the prickly ash tree. They have a bitter flavor and leave a numbing rather than a burning sensation on the tongue.

Tamarind: the brown sticky pulp of the bean-like seed pod of the tamarind tree, used in Southern Indian, Southeast Asian, and Latin American cooking as a souring agent. The pulp is usually diluted with water and strained before using. Pods are available in Latin markets, with blocks of dried pulp in Asian markets.

Tiger lily buds: also called golden needles, these dried unopened flower buds of the tiger lily have a distinct musty flavor and chewy texture.

Tofu (bean curd): the curdled, cheese-like preparation made from soybean milk, tofu is a source of protein in Asian cooking; sold in flat cakes, or blocks that are soft, firm, or extra firm. Store tofu, covered with water, in the refrigerator.

Tree ears: also known as wood ears and cloud ears, this dried fungus has little flavor but a good crunch; it is used in soups and stews.

Wasabi: the greenish flesh of a Japanese horseradish root, it is dried and sold as a powder.

Water chestnut: walnut-sized bulb of an Asian water plant that resembles a regular chestnut with its outer brown layer. Once peeled, the flesh is crisp and sweet, used in stir-fried dishes or eaten as a snack; available fresh, or canned, whole or sliced.

HOW-TO BOXES

In each of the recipes in Asian Cooking you'll find pictures of all the techniques used. However, some basic preparations appear in a number of recipes, and they are shown in extra detail in these special "how-to" boxes:

ASIAN COOKING AND YOUR HEALTH

The healthful properties of Asian cuisine are renowned. Most of the dishes presented in this volume are by nature low in fat and high in complex carbohydrates; only a few – those that are deep-fried or rich in coconut milk for example – are high in fat. Cooking methods, such as stir-frying, broiling, and steaming, keep food moist and flavorful with little or no extra fat being added.

The composition of a typical Asian meal stresses rice, noodles, and fresh vegetables as much as it does meat, poultry, and seafood, balancing their higher levels of cholesterol and saturated fat. Another frequent source of protein in Asian cooking is bean curd, which is a complete protein with little fat and, like vegetables and grains, it has no cholesterol at all.

INDEX

ACKNOWLEDGMENTS

Photographer David Murray
Jules Selmes
Photographer's Assistant Steven Head

Chef Eric Treuille
Cookery Consultant Elaine Ngan
Home Economist Sarah Lowman

US Editor Jeanette Mall

Typesetting Linda Parker
Text film by Disc to Print (UK) Ltd

Production Consultant Lorraine Baird

*Anne Willan would like to thank
Martha Holmberg, Lucy Wing, and
the staff at Carroll & Brown in London
for their vital help in writing this book
and testing the recipes, aided by
La Varenne's editors and trainees*